THE LOST CAPITAL OF BYZANTIUM

THE LOST CAPITAL OF BYZANTIUM

The History of Mistra and the Peloponnese

Steven Runciman

Foreword by John Freely

Harvard University Press
Cambridge, Massachusetts
2009

Copyright © 1980, 2009 Steven Runciman
Foreword copyright © 2009 John Freely

First paperback edition published by Tauris Parke Paperbacks,
an imprint of I.B.Tauris & Co Ltd in the United Kingdom.

First published in the United Kingdom in 1980 by Thames and Hudson Ltd
as *Mistra: Byzantine Capital of the Peloponnese*

ISBN: 978-0-674-03405-1

Cataloging-in-Publication data for this book is available from the Library of
Congress

Printed and bound in the United Kingdom by CPI Antony Rowe, Chippenham,
Wiltshire, UK

Contents

List of Illustrations

Maps drawn by Hanni Bailey

*To the Proedros
and the citizens of Mistra
in gratitude*

Foreword

I REMEMBER my first sight of Mistra in the spring of 1973, when we drove through the mountains of the Peloponnesus to find the ruins of the city that was once the capital of the Byzantine Despotate of the Morea, one of the last outposts of Byzantium. We finally reached the site an hour or so before sunset, when we saw the conical hill crowned with the walls and towers of a crusader castle, with the ruins of the Palace of the Despots and a score of Byzantine churches clustering on the western slope below. The ghost city was shaded by spectral cypresses, the surrounding Vale of Sparta embowered in olive groves and fruit orchards, five snow-covered peaks of Mount Tagetus looming above the abandoned medieval capital to which we were making a pilgrimage.

Seven years later I read Sir Steven Runciman's book on Mistra, which I wished I had with me when I first visited the site, because it told me much about the place and its history that I had not known before, evoking its past and bringing the city to life in a way that no historical text or guide-book could possibly do. This quality was remarked upon by Gore Vidal after finishing Runciman's *A History of the Crusades*, when he remarked that 'To read a historian like Sir Steven Runciman is to be reminded that history is a literary art quite equal to that of the novel.' And so I was particularly pleased to learn that *Lost Capital of Byzantium* is being reissued, for it is a unique classic that should remain in print as a tribute to its author and his role in reviving interest in Byzantine culture. As he wrote in his own preface to *Lost Capital of Byzantium*: 'It is not a guidebook, nor just an essay in appreciation. I have attempted to give a full history of Mistra, to explain how it came into being, to tell of its importance in the last two centuries of the medieval era, and to trace the sadder story of its long decline.'

This history begins early in the thirteenth century when Geoffrey de Villehardouin, a French crusader who had carved out a kingdom in the Peloponnesus, erected a palace in the Vale of Sparta. His son

William built a fortress above the vale on a spur of Mount Taygetus, and the walled town that developed around it came to be called Mistra. When William was captured by the Byzantines in 1261 he was forced to surrender Mistra to the emperor Mchael VIII Palaeologus.

Mistra flourished under Byzantine rule and in 1348 it became the capital of the Despotate of the Morea, as the Peloponnesus was known at the time, ruled by Michael Cantacuzenus, son of the emperor John VI. Constantine XI Dragases, the last Emperor of Byzantium, was Despot of the Morea when he succeeded to the throne in 1449, four years before Constantinople fell to the Ottoman Turks. Mistra itself held out until 1461, one of the last two fragments of Byzantium to fall to the Turks, followed by Trebizond the year afterwards.

During the first half of the fourteenth century Mistra became an intellectual centre of the Byzantine Empire, which flourished in a last renaissance during the two centuries before its fall. Mistra's cultural preeminence stemmed from George Gemistus Plethon, the greatest philosopher of the late Byzantine era, who lived there during most of the period 1407–52, his presence attracting many scholars to the city. Plethon, who was called 'the second Plato', was directly influential in bringing the revived Hellenic culture of Byzantium to the West, sparking the Italian renaissance.

Mistra declined under Ottoman rule, and then in 1770 it was sacked by the Turks after it had been occupied by the Russians. Then in 1824, during the Greek War of Independence, it was sacked again by Ibrahim Pasha, son of Mehmet Ali, the Ottoman viceroy of Egypt, who left the town a smouldering ruin, its surviving people scattered throughout the surrounding communities of Laconia.

After the establishment of the Greek Kingdom in 1832 the government decided to refound the ancient city of Sparta as the administrative centre of Laconia. The former residents of Mistra for the most part resettled in Sparta, leaving the medieval city abandoned except for the southern part of the Exokhorion, or Outer Town, which, as Runciman writes, 'survived to become the small and pleasant town known as Mistra'.

During the past century the Greek government has restored the surviving Byzantine monuments of Mistra and their works of art. Mistra is now a unique monument of Byzantine civilization, preserved as it was at the end of its golden age, dominated by the mighty ramparts of the Villehardouin castle and the surrounding walls of the Kastro, the upper town, a lower line of walls encircling the Mesochorion, or middle town, on the lower slope of the hill. The enormous shell of the Palace of the Despots stands between the upper and middle towns, and scattered on the slope above and below it are the clustered domes of fifteen

Byzantine churches and two monasteries, some of them almost perfectly preserved. And, as Runciman writes, 'as one wanders through the ruined streets and alleyways one begins to see what must have been the great houses of the nobility, the poorer houses, the shops and the barracks, though much remains unidentified.'

One of the restored monuments is the Metropolitan church of St. Demetrius, where Constantine XI Dragases was crowned emperor on 6 January 1449, the place of his coronation marked by a marble stone carved with the double eagle of the Palaeologus dynasty, the enduring symbol of Byzantium. He departed for Constantinople a few weeks after the ceremony, leaving his brothers Demetrius and Thomas to serve jointly as Despots of the Morea. Constantine's reign ended on 29 May 1453, when he died defending Constantinople on the day that it fell to the Turks under Sultan Mehmet II, who within the next nine years would conquer all that still remained of the Byzantine empire.

Runciman evokes the vanished glory of medieval Mistra in the last paragraph of his epilogue, weaving it seamlessly into a vision of the modern town as he himself saw it in 1930, 'journeying on foot, as we did in those days when I was young'.

> The old city is deserted now, except for the kindly nuns who maintain, in the convent of the Pantanassa, the eternal traditions of the Orthodox faith ... But for those to whom history is not just a matter of dry and dusty records, the imagination offers a splendid choice, whether it be of warriors or artists, of gracious ladies or learned philosophers, of the Villehardouin lords revelling in the loveliness of the countryside ... or just of the simple craftsmen and artisans, and the peasants coming up to the marketplace, whose descendants we may still see driving their goats through the steep and narrow alleys, while behind them are the peaks and chasms of Taygetus and spread out before them the incomparable beauty of the hollow vale of Sparta.

Such is Sir Steven Runciman's *Lost Capital of Byzantium*, a superb book about a last remnant of Byzantium that lives again through his evocative history. Runciman dedicated the book to the mayor and people of the modern town, and they in turn named a street in his memory. And now his book has been reissued, and so a new generation of readers will be introduced to the vanished world of Byzantium which he revived through his histories.

John Freely, Istanbul

Preface

FIFTY YEARS have passed since first I came to Mistra, journeying on foot, as we did in those days when I was young. From that moment the enchantment of the place has held me, to be enhanced by every later visit; and more recently the kindness of the modern Mistra, the friendly town that stands on the site of the old city's furthest suburb, has strengthened my bonds. This book is intended as a gesture of gratitude for all that I owe to Mistra and to its people.

It is not a guidebook, nor just an essay in appreciation. I have attempted to give a full history of Mistra, to explain how it came into being, to tell of its importance in the last two centuries of the medieval era, and to trace the sadder story of its long decline. Mistra cannot claim the venerable age of most of the great cities of Europe. It was founded only some seven and a half centuries ago, and the days of its glory lasted for less than two centuries. A century and a half has passed since its final destruction. Yet while it existed it was a focal point. The history of Mistra cannot be understood apart from the whole history of the Peloponnese, in which it was set. Its fate was affected also by events further afield, by a battle in northern Macedonia, or by a massacre in Palermo. A history of Mistra must range over many lands.

Orthography presents a constant difficulty. Are we to use the name 'Mistra' rather than 'Myzethra', which seems to have been the earliest form, or 'Misistra', which was the form employed by most early Western travellers, or 'Mystras', which represents the correct transliteration from the modern Greek? I use the form that seems to be most acceptable to the traveller of today. Are we to call the Peloponnese the Morea, the name that was current in Frankish and Venetian times but usually avoided by the official Greek world? I use either term, according to which sounds the more natural in the context. I cannot claim any consistency in the transliteration of foreign names, but have used whatever form seems to fit most naturally into a book written in English.

In a book such as this, full reference notes would be out of place. I have included at the end a list of the chief original sources and more modern works to which I am beholden; and I have tried to avoid controversial statements that need a detailed argument to support them. I am greatly indebted to Fani-Maria Tzigakou for her valuable help over the illustrations.

It is my hope that this book may encourage civilized travellers to visit Mistra and may perhaps enrich the understanding of those that make the journey.

STEVEN RUNCIMAN

Elshieshields, Dumfriesshire

I The Vale of Sparta

THE BEAUTY of Greece lies mainly in contrast, the contrast between stark promontories and blue sea-gulfs and between barren mountain-sides and fertile valleys. Nowhere is the contrast more marked than in the vale of Sparta, Lacedaemon, the 'hollow land' of the Homeric age. Travellers who take the main road that ran from Tegea in ancient days and runs from Tripolis today, climb up over the spurs of the Parnon range; and suddenly, as they go round a hairpin bend, with the Spartan mountain citadel of Selassia, the guardian of the pass, high above them to the east, there lies below them a valley lush with olive-trees and fruit-trees, with the River Eurotas winding between oleanders and cypresses, and behind the valley, rising steep from the plain, the sternest and most savage of all Greek mountain ranges, Taygetus, with its five peaks, the Five Fingers, covered with snow till late into the summer. In front of the mountain wall, if the morning sun is shining, they will notice a conical hill, dotted with buildings and crowned by a castle. This is Mistra.

From the earliest times the rich plain of Sparta has been a centre of Greek life. It was here in Mycenaean days that Helen, the loveliest of the queens of history, lived and reigned till she eloped to Troy, and it is here that she lies, so tradition says, along with Menelaus, the husband whom she wronged and to whom she returned, together in the mausoleum on the hill top of Therapne. Before Christian saints replaced her, her tomb was a shrine at which one prayed to be granted beautiful children. Later, the Dorians came, to set up in Sparta a state unrivalled in history for its rigidity and its discipline.

The constitution was the work, it was said, of the law-giver Lycurgus, a dim mythical figure who may have lived in the eighth century BC. According to the myth, when he had presented his code to his compatriots he departed for a journey, having made them swear an oath not to alter it till he returned; deliberately he remained in exile and his constitution endured for half a millennium. There were three classes: the Helots, probably the descendants of the old Achaean population – serfs who tilled the land and performed menial tasks for their Spartiate masters; the Paroikoi, the inhabitants of the towns and villages that fell under Spartan domination – farmers and shopkeepers, free men but without any voice in the government; and the Spartiates themselves, who elected their magistrates and the Senate, with two hereditary kings at their head, without any autocratic power but with a certain prestige. The kings would be accepted as leaders in time of war, unless their age or known incompetence made them unsuitable. Except for the elected magistrates and Senators everyone followed his father's profession, as a lawyer or an armourer or a breeder of horses, or whatever it might be. But all were liable to military service. Women enjoyed a freedom remarkable in ancient Greece. They had to bear children for the State, and they had no vote; but they mingled with the men, and in times of war they practically took over the administration. Everything was geared towards military efficiency. Education, even of girls, was primarily militaristic. Weaklings did not exist; unhealthy babies were exposed at once to die on the bleak slopes of Taygetus. It was a community that discouraged individual effort. It produced no important works of art and very little literature or music, apart from choral songs. But it offered security and stability. Sparta was the only city in Greece that had no need of fortification. The whole valley was protected by mountain walls, Taygetus on the west, Parnon on the north and east, and the lower hills of the Vardounokhoria protecting the access from the sea to the south; and the prowess of the Spartan army provided an outer wall. To later philhellenes, dazzled by the superb achievements of Athenian genius, Sparta has always seemed deplorable in comparison with free democratic Athens. They forget that Athenian democracy was made possible by a vast slave population and that Athenian women were little better off than those slaves, while its individualism led to faction and turbulence and disaster. Many Athenians looked with envy at the steadiness of Spartan life.

But in the end Spartan rigidity broke down. Her very victories over Athens brought in the corrupting influence of rich booty. Her military machine declined; and the other Greek states, which had hated her for centuries, united against her. In the fourth century BC the Spartans saw for the first time enemy troops come into their valley and attack their unwalled city. Attempts either to restore or to liberalize the old constitution all ended in failure. In the middle of the second century Sparta fell, after a brief struggle, under the domination of Rome.

Greece had already become a backwater, away from the mainstream of history. Her enterprising citizens moved away to the great cities of the Hellenistic world, or to Rome itself, or to the splendid capital that Constantine the Great was to build on the shores of the Bosphorus. Under the Roman emperors the Greek cities were little more than museums. In Sparta the fierce contests which had initiated boys into manhood were now enacted before tourists in a theatre. The severity had vanished from Spartan life; the valley of the Eurotas was noted for its indolent, easy-going luxury. The ghost of Helen had triumphed over the ghost of Lycurgus.

The coming of Christianity brought a tightening of morals. But it seems that the Spartans were not over-eager to embrace the new religion. It is not till well into the fifth century AD that we hear definitely of a bishop of Lacedaemon – for the Church reverted to the older and more melodious name for the city. By the end of the fifth century all signs of paganism were gone. The temples were deserted or had been transformed into churches. The games and contests were abandoned; and expectant mothers no longer climbed up the hill of Therapne to pray at the tomb of Helen. But already the tranquillity of life in the valley had been interrupted. In 376 the Imperial government allowed the barbarian nation of the Visigoths to cross the Danube into the Empire. Nineteen years later, under their restless leader Alaric, angry that they had been given no lands in which to settle, they forced their way into the Greek peninsula. Athens was spared, as Alaric, good Christian though he professed himself to be, had a vision of the goddess Athena and the hero Hercules guarding the walls. So they pressed on across the Isthmus of Corinth into the Peloponnese, pillaging as they passed, and eventually in the late summer of 395 they fell upon defenceless Sparta. For the first time in its history the city was sacked. It seems that Alaric contemplated the establishment of a kingdom for himself in the Peloponnese; but after a few months the approach of an Imperial army induced him to move northward, into Illyria, and to resume the restless career that was to bring fire and the sword into Italy and to the city of Rome itself.

Peace returned to the vale of Sparta for nearly two centuries. But confidence had been lost. Walls were built at last to protect the city itself. These centuries saw a decline in the whole prosperity of the Greek peninsula. With the triumph of Christianity the cities of Greece lost their ancient prestige and their more enterprising citizens left for livelier provinces. Trade across the Mediterranean now passed Greece by, and there was little industry there. The weight of Imperial taxation, particularly in the reign of the Emperor Justinian, fell heavily on a province that had few natural resources. The Emperors' attention was occupied by worries along their frontiers or by dreams of reconquest of Western provinces from the barbarians. But worse was to come.

In the last decades of the sixth century, when the Empire was distracted by a bitter war against the Persians and the huge Turkic empire of the Avars was pressing into the Balkan peninsula, a new racial element made its way into Greece. Since early in the century the Slavs had been pouring into the Balkan peninsula. Now, partly encouraged by the Avars and partly to escape from direct Avar domination, parties of them came down into Greece. Before the end of the century they were crowding into the Peloponnese; and in the first decade of the seventh century, when the incompetent Phocas was reigning in Constantinople, their numbers so vastly increased that it seemed to alarmed onlookers that the whole of Greece was in the hands of barbarian and pagan Slavs.

The pleasant vale of Sparta was to their liking; and the Greek inhabitants fled. Many fled southward, to the wild hills of the Mani peninsula, where they revived the stern martial virtues of the Spartan of old. Some fled to coastal towns which the Slavs were unable to capture, in particular to the fortress rock of Monemvasia, jutting out into the Aegean Sea. Many more fled across the sea, westward to Sicily, to found a new Lacedaemon, which they called more briefly Demona, in what seemed to be a safer land. Some must have stayed, to intermarry with the invaders and to bring them a modicum of culture. For two centuries the vale of Sparta, and the mountains around, were in the hands of the barbarians; and Christianity and the cultured standards of Byzantine life well-nigh disappeared.

The recovery of Greece for the Greeks began in the last years of the eighth century, under the Empress Irene, herself an Athenian by birth. But the Peloponnese was rescued under her successor, Nicephorus I. A series of campaigns undertaken by his governor of the Peloponnese, Leo Sclerus, drove the Slavs into the mountains and cleared the valleys for the Greeks to return to them. As so many Greeks had emigrated during the Slav occupation, the Emperor found it necessary to bring in settlers from other parts of the Empire. It seems that the colonists whom he sent to the vale of Sparta came mostly from Asia Minor, Greeks, together with a few Armenians, while many of the descendants of the earlier Spartans must have returned to their homes. In about 810 a bishopric was re-established in Sparta – the Bishopric of Lacedaemon – under the authority of the Metropolitanate of Patras.

The vale was now again to enjoy a period of comparative peace. The Slav tribes which had retired into the Taygetus range and into the

Arcadian mountains still occasionally tried to raid the valleys; and now and then military expeditions had to be sent against them, to restore obedience and to extract from them such meagre tribute as they could afford to pay. Soon they were persuaded to adopt Christianity, chiefly owing to the efforts of a tenth-century saint, Nikon, surnamed Metanoeite, or 'Repent ye', a man of Armenian origin, born at Argos, who tramped round the Laconian mountains firmly preaching the Gospels. He was a man of forceful personality, but unattractively intolerant. When Sparta was smitten by the plague he refused to enter the city until all the Jews who had settled there in recent years had been expelled. Then he came; and the plague ceased at once. When a little later Bulgarians threatened the Peloponnese, the governor of the province summoned him to Corinth. The prestige of his presence there restored morale; and the Bulgarians prudently withdrew. He was an indefatigable founder of churches, especially in or near to Sparta. On his death he was canonized; and the grateful Spartans adopted him as their patron saint. He had certainly made the city the liveliest religious centre in the province: though it was not till 1081, about a century after his death, that the Bishopric of Lacedaemon was raised to Metropolitan rank.

The vale enjoyed a growing prosperity throughout the tenth and eleventh centuries. The Slav tribes of Taygetus, known now as the Milengi and the Ezerites, were no longer a threat. An attempted rising in about 925 had been suppressed by military action; and, thanks to St Nikon and his disciples, they were now Christian. So long as they paid their tribute regularly they were allowed autonomy, under a district officer appointed by the governor of the Peloponnese. The Greeks of the Mani and the Tzakones – probably of mixed Greek and Slav origin – of the Parnon range, were now pious and fairly orderly citizens. There were Spartans wealthy enough to visit the Imperial capital. The lovely Empress Theophano, wife of Romanus II, came from Sparta. Later gossip declared that her father was a Spartan innkeeper. But if he was, the hotel trade must have been flourishing; for he could afford to send her to Constantinople, where she moved in circles frequented by the young Emperor. If his father, Constantine VII, was distressed when the youth fell in love with her, it was only because he was negotiating to betroth his son to a German princess, Hedwig of Bavaria, niece of the Western Emperor Otho I, a lady who, later, as Duchess of Swabia, became one of the great termagants of medieval history. But Constantine did not forbid the marriage with Theophano. Some fifteen years later she was an accomplice in the murder of her second husband, Nicephorus II, a grim general whom she had married to preserve her sons' throne; and rumours began to circulate that she must have been responsible for the deaths of Constantine VIII and Romanus II. The accusation is unjustified. Constantine was an ageing man of very poor health, while the death of Romanus endangered her whole career. Her son, Basil II, was the greatest of Byzantine warrior–emperors. It was perhaps from his mother's Spartan ancestors that he inherited his austere disregard of culture and comfort and his devotion to military prowess.

Sparta and the neighbouring Laconian lands were not exposed to direct harm in the wars against the Turks and against the Normans that nearly wrecked Byzantium in the later eleventh century. But prosperity declined. In the chaos piracy returned to the Aegean Sea, and trade suffered. The taxes imposed by the emperors of the twelfth century were higher than ever before; and the peasants could not pay them. As had happened already elsewhere in the Empire they were obliged to hand their lands over to some magnate who could afford the burden, or afford to defy the tax-collectors, and to become his employees. By the later years of the twelfth century the Peloponnese, except for the tribal areas, was in the hands of a few great families, who paid little respect to the Imperial government, even when their members were appointed to local posts of authority; and, indeed, the Imperial government of the last two decades of the century, under incompetent emperors of the Angelus dynasty, was deserving of no respect.

In Sparta, which the writers of the time now always called Lacedaemon or Lacedemonia, the dominant family was the Chamareti. We know the names of three of them, Michael, his nephew John and John's brother Leo, who was ruling the whole province of Laconia, with the title of *proedros*, at the time of the Fourth Crusade. The Peloponnese, or the Morea, to give it a name that was coming into popular use, had been bypassed by the earlier Crusades. The invasion of Greece by Roger II of Sicily in 1146 spared it after his troops had failed to capture the fortress of Monemvasia. No one in the peninsula noticed when in the summer of 1203 the great army of the Fourth Crusade sailed in Venetian ships round the coast on its way to Constantinople. No one realized that the simple greed of the Crusaders and the calculated greed of the Venetians were to result in the capture and looting of the Imperial capital. News of the disaster reached the Peloponnese in the late spring of 1204. There was consternation and apprehension; but no one in the vale of Sparta foresaw that this was to lead to the two most brilliant centuries in the history of Lacedaemon.

II The Coming of the Franks

IN MARCH 1204, a month before they captured the Imperial city, the knights of the Fourth Crusade and their Venetian allies began to discuss how they would divide the Empire which they hoped soon to conquer. The treaty of partition, which listed the territories which were to be allotted to the new Latin emperor, the leading Crusader lords and the Venetians, was signed in October. Few treaties have been so impractical. The emperor, Count Baldwin of Flanders, had to share Constantinople itself with the Venetians, who were to have three-eighths of it; and they also shared the province of Thrace with him. Most of the lands assigned to him were in Asia. None of them had yet been and few ever were to be conquered by the Latins. The signatories timorously avoided the question of Thessalonica, which had been claimed and occupied by the Marquis of Montferrat, the Count of Flanders' chief rival on the Crusade. Lesser lords were given lands in the Greek peninsula and the islands, most of them still to be conquered. It was Venice that did best. After centuries of trading in Byzantine waters the Venetians knew what would be of use to them. In fact, they demanded and obtained far more than they intended to occupy. Besides their share of Constantinople and Thrace they were to receive the whole of western Greece, up to the dividing Pindus range, and practically the whole of the Peloponnese, including Lacedaemon and the province of Laconia. Most of this territory was unconquered; and Venice had no desire to spend money and time on conquering lands that might be awkward and expensive to administer. But it might be valuable to have a recorded legal right to them.

Despite the reluctance of the Venetians to take over their allotted lands, the Peloponnese was not left in peace for long. The local Greek lords had hoped to enjoy independence. The most energetic of them, Leo Sgouros, lord of Nauplia, had already, even before the fall of Constantinople, been planning to build up a principality in Greece. He had occupied Argos and then Corinth, with its impregnable citadel of

Acrocorinth. In the summer of 1204 he marched on Athens and captured the lower city, though the acropolis held out against him under its distinguished archbishop, Michael Acominatus. By September 1204, Sgouros had taken Thebes in Boeotia and had reached Larissa in Thessaly. There he met some distinguished refugees from Constantinople, including the former Emperor Alexius III and his daughter Eudocia, widow of Alexius V Murzuphlus. He hastened to marry Eudocia, to give an air of legitimacy to his power. The Peloponnesian lords, such as Leo Chamaterus in Sparta, watched his advance with contentment. He did not interfere with their independence, and he would, they thought, serve as protection against a Frankish advance.

Their hopes were to be disappointed. Sgouros, for all his enterprise and personal courage, was loathed by the Greek populace for his savagery; and he was as extortionate as any Imperial tax-collector. His army was small and unreliable. When at the end of September he learnt that a great Frankish army was marching down from the north he moved back to the Pass of Thermopylae. Then, considering that it would be pointless to emulate the Spartans of long ago, he retreated to the Isthmus of Corinth.

The Frankish army was led by Boniface, Marquis of Montferrat. He had hoped in vain to become emperor at Constantinople but had established himself instead as ruler of Thessalonica; and he intended to set up Crusader states in Greece that should owe fealty to him, rather than to the emperor, Baldwin of Flanders, or to the Venetians. Of all the Crusader leaders Boniface was the most acceptable to the Greeks. He came from a small principality in Lombardy, but he was rich and well-connected, the cousin of both the King of France and the German Emperor. As an Italian he seemed preferable to the crude, uncivilized knights from beyond the Alps. Moreover, his family had many connections with the East. His eldest brother had been the son-in-law of the Emperor Manuel Comnenus and had been a popular viceroy in Thessalonica. He himself, soon after the fall of Constantinople, had married the widow of the Emperor Isaac Angelus, Margaret of Hungary, who had come to Constantinople as a young girl and had many friends there. A number of Greeks joined his banner, including a bastard prince of the Angelus family, Michael: who, however, left the army in Thessaly to go westward to Epirus, to fish in troubled waters there, taking most of the Greek troops with him.

The defection in no way troubled Boniface, who marched on, assigning fiefs to trusted colleagues as he advanced. Sgouros found it impossible to hold the Isthmus and retired to his citadel of

Acrocorinth. Boniface left troops to besiege him there and went on to attack his other castles, at Argos and at Nauplia. Both were formidable fortresses; and Boniface did not have enough men to try to storm them. He waited below, to blockade the enemy till they should be starved into surrender.

So long as these three castles held up the Crusading army, Leo Chamaterus in the vale of Sparta and the petty lords who were his neighbours could hope to rule their lands in peace. They had now, too, a potential protector. Michael Angelus had gone off to Epirus on hearing that the local governor, his cousin Senacherim, was in difficulties. He arrived to find Senacherim recently assassinated. He promptly married his widow and took over the government. He was able and energetic, and well-liked by the local population. Within a year he was master of all western Greece, from Dyrrhachium to the Gulf of Corinth. This was an area in which the Crusaders were uninterested; it had been allotted to Venice by the partition treaty but the Venetians did nothing until Michael was well established. Then they demanded that he accept their overlordship and open his cities to their merchants. It suited him well. The overlordship was nominal but gave him some protection against his neighbours; and Venetian trade brought prosperity to his people. He began to see himself as champion of the Greeks in Greece.

Danger came to the Peloponnese from an unexpected quarter. Among the knights who took the Cross to go on the Fourth Crusade were two lords from Champagne, the Marshal William of Villehardouin and his nephew Geoffrey. William travelled with the main expedition and was to become its chief chronicler. Geoffrey was late in setting out and decided to go with his small company straight to Palestine. It was only when he arrived there that he heard of the diversion of the Crusade to Constantinople; and he seems to have received a personal message from his uncle urging him to come and share in the rich spoils to be won in Byzantine lands. So, after a brief pilgrimage to the Holy Places, he took passage along with a few fellow-Crusaders in a small squadron that was sailing to the Bosphorus. It was now well into the autumn; and the ships were scattered by a storm. The one in which Geoffrey and his handful of followers were travelling was driven westward and put in for refuge at the port of Methone, near the south-western tip of the Peloponnese. The local Greek lord was eager to extend his lands at the expense of his neighbours. He invited Geoffrey to help him, promising him a rich reward. There was little point in trying to sail on to Constantinople in the treacherous winter weather. So Geoffrey accepted the offer, and soon found out how easy it would be for a few well-armed Western soldiers to conquer territory in the Peloponnese. The local Greeks were quite unused to fighting. Their weapons and equipment were scanty and out of date; and they felt little loyalty to their rulers, not caring which lord it was who was trying to exploit them. It was only from the garrisons of the few fortified castles and from one or two mountain tribes that invaders would meet with any strong resistance.

Geoffrey spent the winter conquering the province of Messenia for his patron. But in the spring of 1205 the lord of Methone died, and his son dismissed Geoffrey without giving him his promised reward. Geoffrey's followers were too few for him to make an effective protest. So, knowing now that Boniface of Montferrat was in the Peloponnese laying siege to Nauplia, he set out with his troop to ride across the mountains to join him. After six adventurous days they reached the Frankish camp. There Geoffrey met an old friend from Champagne, William of Champlitte. William's father had been the son of a countess of Champagne but had been repudiated as a bastard by the count and had therefore only inherited his mother's lands of Champlitte. But many nobles of Champagne, the Villehardouins amongst them, thought that injustice had been done and regarded the lord of Champlitte as their true overlord. So, though William was only a younger son, Geoffrey felt a feudal allegiance to him. William was ambitious; and when Geoffrey told him that there were rich lands in the Morea which a small professional army easily could conquer he listened with eagerness. Boniface gave his approval to the scheme and allowed William to withdraw his personal troops. It was agreed that William would hold any conquered lands under the suzerainty of Boniface, and Geoffrey would pay homage to William for any lands allotted to him.

The small expedition set out in April 1205. It numbered about a hundred knights and four or five hundred other ranks. It set out northward, and as it passed by Corinth a number of troops from the army besieging Acrocorinth broke away to join it. Then it marched westward along the north coast of the Peloponnese, meeting with no resistance and leaving small garrisons in the larger towns. At Patras it turned southward, through Elis. The local capital, Andravida, was unfortified; and the leading citizens welcomed the invaders. As the expedition moved on, only the castle of Arkadia, the modern Kyparissia, held out against it. Troops were left to blockade it, while William and Geoffrey entered Messenia. The lord of Methone fled to the hills; and the Franks occupied Methone and Corone, then skirted the Gulf of Messenia to Kalamata. The town fell, but the castle resisted them.

Kalamata lay just over the Taygetus mountains from the vale of Sparta; and Leo Chamaterus, lord of Lacedemonia, was seriously alarmed. He sent messages to the lords of Nikli and Veligosti, whose lands commanded the northern approaches to the vale from the centre of the Peloponnese. All of them appealed for help to the one Greek potentate left in Eastern Europe, Michael Angelus of Epirus, to whom the garrison at Arkadia had also applied. Michael was glad to intervene in the Peloponnese. He set out at once with a company of light horsemen. The Franks besieging Acrocorinth allowed him to pass unchallenged through the Isthmus. In the centre of the peninsula he was joined by levies raised by the lords of Lacedemonia, Nikli and Veligosti. It was at the head of some five thousand men that he marched into Messenia to meet the invaders. He came upon them at an olive-grove called Koundoura.

William and Geoffrey had only some six hundred soldiers; but they were all professionals, well trained and well equipped. Many men of the original expedition had been left to garrison conquered cities, but it seems that driblets of men had joined it from time to time, coming from the detachments engaged in the boring task of blockading Sgouros's castles. There were also a number of Greeks who were ready to act as guides and scouts for the Franks. In contrast, the Greek lords' levies were composed of men unaccustomed to war and with little liking for it. At the first charge of the heavy Frankish cavalry they scattered. Many were slain. The survivors fled; and Michael's light cavalry could not rally them. Soon the Greek lords were galloping back to their cities and the Despot and his horsemen back across the Isthmus of Corinth.

The victory gave to William of Champlitte mastery over the Peloponnese. Before the end of 1205 he received letters from the Pope addressing him as 'Prince of all Achaea'. The name 'Achaea', though it was now taken, like 'Morea', to include the whole Peloponnese, originally designated only the western parts of the peninsula. So the title was for the moment more accurate than William may have realized. He still had to occupy the eastern districts. But, as they could do him no harm, he took Geoffrey's advice and did not march on Laconia, making sure, instead, of his hold on the west. The castle of Arkadia was starved into submission. He then attacked the castle of Araklovon, which commanded the best road into the interior plateau. Its lord, a giant Greek called Doxipatras, refused to surrender it. But his garrison was tiny and could not resist the Frankish assault. Doxipatras was killed; and his lovely daughter, Maria, flung herself from the castle walls to avoid the amorous attentions of the conqueror.

About the same time Geoffrey of Villehardouin stormed the castle of Kalamata. William assigned the town to him, together with the whole district of Messenia. It was at Kalamata that Geoffrey made his residence. He was not allowed to enjoy his whole appanage for long. The Venetians, to whom the Peloponnese had been allotted in the partition treaty, decided that, now that the province had been conquered by the Franks, the time had come to claim the parts that would be of use to them. In 1206 a Venetian squadron landed troops at Methone and at Corone, ejecting Geoffrey's small garrison. The fortifications of Methone that he had recently built were destroyed; but Corone was developed to be a fortified harbour at which Venetian ships could call for water and provisions when voyaging further to the East. Geoffrey made no protest. He may have considered that there were potential advantages in a Venetian presence in the peninsula. To recompense him for his loss William added the castle of Arkadia to his fief. By 1207 Geoffrey felt secure enough to summon his wife and his son from France. Next year a second son was born at Kalamata and christened William.

By that time Geoffrey was ruler of Achaea. At the end of 1208 William of Champlitte learnt that his elder brother had died without issue in France. To secure the family lands for his young children William was obliged as next heir to appear and claim them himself within a year and a day. Early in the next year he summoned vassals and followers to Andravida, which he had made his capital. A commission composed of two bishops, two bannerets and four Greek lawyers divided the peninsula, including the still unconquered districts, into fiefs, each knight's share being calculated upon the number of his followers and his ability to administer and defend the territory. Lacedemonia, however, was to be reserved for the Prince. William appointed his bastard nephew, Hugh of Champlitte, to act as his bailli, or regent, in his absence. He then set out for France. He never arrived there but died of fever in Apulia on the journey. His bailli barely survived him. A new bailli was needed. As Geoffrey held by far the largest fief and was known to have master-minded the conquest, and as he was also liked by the conquered Greeks, the barons elected him without hesitation. In March 1210, having waited the customary year and a day for some member of the Champlitte family to come to claim the inheritance, he took the title of Prince. A later legend told of a certain Robert of Champlitte who set out for Greece on behalf of the family but was so ingeniously delayed by Geoffrey's machinations at every stage of the journey that he arrived at Andravida just too late to make his claim. But the story is full of inconsistencies and inaccuracies. Robert probably never existed. The only surviving members of the house were two small children who were happy to remain in Champagne.

Geoffrey's first action as bailli was to confirm the barons of Achaea in their fiefs. He then set out to occupy the unconquered parts of the peninsula. First, he marched on Veligosti, which surrendered without a struggle, and then on Nikli, which was more strongly fortified. There the garrison fought fiercely for a week before it surrendered. The road was now open for him to enter the vale of Sparta.

Leo Chamaterus had long expected the attack. The walls of Lacedemonia were in good condition; but the Lacedemonians were half-hearted in their defence, and he knew that no one would come to his rescue. After five days of resistance he handed the city over to Geoffrey and was allowed to retire to a country estate.

The vale of Sparta was at its loveliest in the early spring weather; and Geoffrey was enchanted by it. He built himself a palace on the banks of the Eurotas – probably outside the city walls, but no trace of it is left. It was his favourite residence. Andravida remained the administrative capital of the principality; and Nikli, from its central situation, became a convenient location for special assemblies of the baronage. But it was in Lacedemonia, La Crémonie, as they called it, that the Villehardouins made their home.

The rest of Laconia was quickly overrun; and the castles round the valley, Nikli to the north, Geraki on the east and Passava in the Mani, were allotted to trusted vassals. But Geoffrey kept the valley itself as the princely domain.

The wild tribes that inhabited the neighbouring mountains, the Milengi of Taygetus, the Tzakones of Parnon, and the Maniots in the south, were cowed into nominal submission to the Prince, though none of his officials would venture into their territory without a fully armed escort. The only possessions left to the Greeks in the Peloponnese were now the fortress of Monemvasia, on its great rock jutting out into the sea off the south-east coast, and the three remnants of Leo Sgouros's dominion, the citadels of Corinth, Argos and Nauplia. Monemvasia was ruled by three hereditary archons; and its citizens grew rich on piracy, patriotically directed against Frankish shipping. Sgouros's three citadels were less happily placed. Each had been blockaded since 1205. But the blockade was a dreary task. It was no wonder that many of the soldiers would drift off to join the forces of the Prince of Achaea. But, though the besiegers could not prevent supplies and even men from reaching the beleaguered fortresses, the small garrisons were too small to attempt any sortie. In 1208 Leo

Sgouros was driven mad by the strain of having lived for nearly four years cooped up within the walls of Acrocorinth, and leapt on horseback over the precipice that surrounded the citadel, ending as a mangled corpse on the rocks below. But the garrison did not give up. When he heard the news, Michael Angelus of Epirus sent troops southward under his half-brother Theodore. Theodore broke through the blockade and reinforced all three castles, taking up his own residence in Acrocorinth.

In April 1210, Geoffrey of Villehardouin set out with all his available troops to press forward the siege of Acrocorinth. He had barely arrived there when he received a summons to meet the Latin Emperor of Constantinople at Ravenika in Thessaly.

Since Geoffrey had arrived in the Peloponnese, the Franks settled further to the east had passed through an unhappy period. After the fall of Constantinople three Greek succession states had emerged. There was Michael Angelus's Despotate in Epirus in the west. Far to the east there was the Empire of the Grand Comnenus at Trebizond. In the centre, not far from Constantinople itself, a son-in-law of the Emperor Alexius III, Theodore Lascaris, had established himself in the hallowed city of Nicaea and was soon recognized by most of the Greek world as representing the legitimate Empire. The first Latin emperor of Constantinople, Baldwin of Flanders, was a foolish man. His troops had failed to occupy more than a fringe of Byzantine Asia Minor and were soon on the defensive against the Nicaeans. Then Baldwin had unnecessarily provoked a war against the rising power of Bulgaria in the Balkans; and the Bulgarians had defeated and captured him at the battle of Vernicia in Thrace in February 1206. He died in captivity. Exactly a year later the Bulgarians ambushed and slew his one-time rival, Boniface of Montferrat, King of Thessalonica. The Franks were saved by Baldwin's brother and successor, Henry, the ablest and most attractive of all the Frankish princes in the East. He kept the Greeks of Nicaea and the Bulgarians at bay and made himself popular with his Greek as well as his Frankish subjects. When civil war broke out in Thessalonica on Boniface's death he marched on the city and himself crowned Boniface's young son as king and received his homage. He had now moved into northern Greece to secure the allegiance of the Frankish states that had been set up in Greek territory, which had hitherto regarded the King of Thessalonica as their overlord.

Geoffrey was graciously received by the Emperor, who treated him as the chief of his vassals in Greece and gave him the title of Seneschal of Romania. At Ravenika Geoffrey met a friend whom he had known when they were children together in France, Otho of La Roche, who had acquired the lordship of Athens and Thebes. Otho agreed to help him in the reduction of Acrocorinth. After the meeting at Ravenika was over their two armies marched on Acrocorinth. They blockaded the city so thoroughly now that in the early autumn it was forced to surrender. Just before it fell Theodore Angelus managed to escape with all the city treasures to Argos. There he held out in the citadel, the Larissa, till the summer of 1212, when it, too, was starved into surrender. Once more he escaped himself, but this time without the treasure. The castle at Nauplia had been taken in 1211, with the help of the Venetian fleet. As Geoffrey was always short of manpower, he was glad to assign the three castles to Otho, to hold under him and his heirs.

Venetian help had been forthcoming as a result of a treaty that Geoffrey had made with the Republic immediately after his return from Ravenika. He recognized its possession of Corone and Methone and of the south-west corner of the Peloponnese as far north as the Bay of Pylos. He did homage to the Republic for the whole Peloponnese, but 'without prejudice to his fealty to his lord, the Emperor of Romania'. As a token of his loyalty he had to send three silk robes yearly to Venice, one for the Doge and two for the Church of St Mark. He was to complete the conquest of Laconia and assign a quarter of it to the Republic, a clause that he never fulfilled; nor did he fulfil the clause that as a citizen of the Republic he and his heirs should maintain a residence in Venice. Finally, Venetian merchants were to enjoy free trading rights throughout the principality.

By 1213 Geoffrey was master of the whole Peloponnese, except for the small Venetian province, a few wild mountain valleys and Monemvasia. His dual allegiance to the Emperor at Constantinople and the Venetian Republic sat very lightly on him. Indeed, he suffered greater restraint from the strict feudal constitution of the principality. As prince, he was commander-in-chief and could demand that his feudatories should join him on his campaigns. He could forbid them to leave the country. He could control the marriages of heiresses. He could reallot fiefs that fell vacant. But he was subject to the authority of the High Court of the principality. This was composed of the chief feudatories, the Archbishop of Patras and his bishops and the local Masters of the three great Military Orders, the Templars, the Hospitallers and the Teutonic Knights, all of whom held lands in the Principality. Without the permission of the High Court the Prince could not punish any feudatory who disobeyed him; and, though he was President of the Court, he could be sued before it. He was

The Peloponnese

ECHINADES ISLANDS

P
Gal
Salme
Patras Vostits
A C H A E A Kala
Agia Lavra
Clarenza
Andravida
Chlemoutsi
ZANTE
Akova
Pyrgos
ARO
Alpheus
Karytaina
Siderokastro Veligosti
Gardiki Leo
Arkadia
(Kyparissia)
MESSENIA
Androusa
Kalamat
Navarino
Methone
Corone
V

0   10   20   30   Mls
0 10 20 30 40 50 Km

Cape N

- Salona
C I S

Chalkis

Thebes

B O E O T I A

GULF OF CORINTH

A T T I C A

Sikyon
Acrocorinth
Hexamilion

Corinth

Megara

Athens

SALAMIS

SARONIC GULF

AEGINA

Argos
Nauplia

OIA

Tripolitza
Nikli

PARNON

ion
Arakhova

HYDRA

Sparta TZAKONIA
Mistra
Geraki

Eurotas

LACONIA

Passava
Githion

Monemvasia

MANI

Maina

pan

CYTHERA

responsible for the general administration. But decisions on policy, especially foreign policy, needed the High Court's approval.

At this time there were twelve major fiefs, two of which, Arkadia and Kalamata, were held by Geoffrey himself, while the Archbishop of Patras had six suffragans. The High Court thus numbered twenty persons, not including the prince. Below these chief barons were lesser feudatories, knights with small estates whose relations to the baron were similar to those of the baron to the prince. Amongst them were the Greek lords who had been allowed to keep their lands. These, in fact, formed a separate class, despised by their Frankish neighbours; but its members were often used by the prince and the greater feudatories when dealing with local problems. The towns were administered by local councils, under the strict supervision of the prince or the local lord. At the bottom of the scale were the peasants. Under their previous Greek lords they had been tied to the land. Now their serfdom was legalized. They had no right even to their meagre personal possessions. The produce of their labours, except for what was needed for their bare subsistence, went to the lord. They could be transferred from lord to lord. A free girl who married a serf became a serf; but a serf's daughter who with the lord's permission married a free man thereby won her freedom.

As usually happens in a colonizing society, the authorities at the top were benevolent and considerate towards their native subjects. It was the invaders of lesser rank who were contemptuous and arrogant towards the Greeks. But there were inevitable contacts. The invaders had come without their womenfolk; and only the wealthiest could afford to summon their wives out from the West. The poorer Frankish soldiers, even many of the knights, had to find their wives from amongst the Greeks. This led to the emergence of a half-caste population known as the *gasmoules*. The children of knights and sergeants tended to identify themselves with their fathers' kin, speaking French and adhering to the Latin Church. The children of poorer soldiers were more apt to speak Greek and follow their mothers' religion. But most of them inherited their fathers' taste for fighting. They began to form among the Greeks a warlike element on which the Frankish lords could not wholly rely.

It was, in fact, religion that caused the cleavage in society. The Western clergy who came in with the conquerors were determined to latinize the whole Church. The Orthodox Greek bishops were driven into exile and in their cathedrals there were services with a strange ritual in an alien tongue. Even the monasteries were taken over; and all the ecclesiastical estates passed into Latin hands. Thanks chiefly to

Prince Geoffrey the parish priest was left in comparative peace. He could conduct the liturgy in his traditional way and he was given immunity from taxation. But he was nominally under a Latin superior. He could no longer go for spiritual advice to a bishop of his own faith, nor refresh his knowledge of holy books in the local monastery library. Robbed of its leaders the Orthodox Church in Greece began to lose its cultural standards. But it never lost the allegiance of the people.

In this complicated society Lacedemonia held a special place. The Villehardouins regarded the vale of Sparta as being their personal patrimony, unlike their lands at Kalamata and Arkadia, which were fiefs of the principality. Though Geoffrey had installed feudatories in the castles that surrounded the valley, he seems to have discouraged Franks from settling in the valley itself. He spent there as much time as he could. His household was full of Greek clerks and stewards who enjoyed his goodwill and were protected by him from the insolence of the Franks. The frequent presence of his court in the city brought it new life. The bazaars flourished. The shopkeepers found rich clients in the Prince's entourage and among the lords who came to pay him their respects. Life was not too hard for the peasants living on the fertile princely estates in the valley. But there could not be complete contentment. Prince Geoffrey, for all his benevolence towards the Greeks, was a loyal son of the Latin Church. He could not refuse to let a Latin bishop take over the diocese. The Orthodox bishop had been driven out, and Latin priests now stalked arrogantly through the streets, stirring up resentment.

Nevertheless, Geoffrey's Greek subjects were aware of his goodwill. He was almost as popular with them as with the Frankish knights whom he had led to victory. When he died in 1218 the mourning throughout the Peloponnese was deep and sincere.

III The Foundation of Mistra

LIFE in the latter years of Prince Geoffrey's reign in the Peloponnese had been tranquil and prosperous. The only political struggle within the principality had been caused by the Prince's determination to make the Latin bishops contribute from their wealth to the princely exchequer; and that was a struggle which his Greek subjects could regard with equanimity. The same peace was maintained during the reign of his heir, his elder son Geoffrey II. Geoffrey II was held to be the richest and most brilliant prince of his time. He was aged about thirty at the time of his accession and had been married for ten years to the sister of the last two Latin emperors of Constantinople. The Princess Agnes was a shadowy figure, who probably shared the feck-lessness that characterized her two brothers; but she was doubtless a good hostess. Her husband was certainly a splendid host. His court was famed for its feasts and its tourneys. The Prince maintained eight fully armed knights as his personal bodyguard; and knights from the West who had taken the vow to go to the rescue of the dying Kingdom of Jerusalem or the dying Latin Empire of Constantinople often paused on their way in Achaea and remained there in the service of the Prince. Like his father, Geoffrey II loved his palace at La Crémonie, or Lacedemonia, best of all his residences. It was the scene of the grandest festivities.

For all his love of splendour, Geoffrey II was an able and conscienti-ous administrator. Perfect order was kept throughout his dominions; and his agents went regularly round his vassals' courts to make sure that they governed justly and did not exploit the Greeks. He was also a good soldier and a superb diplomat. In 1236 his fleet, under his leadership, saved Constantinople from a combined attack by the Greeks and the Bulgarians. In return his brother-in-law, the Emperor Baldwin II, to whom he gave a yearly subsidy, allotted to him the suzerainty over the Aegean Archipelago and Euboea as well as the lordship of the great castle of Boudenitsa, situated near to the Pass of

Thermopylae. Geoffrey also was recognized as overlord of the Duchy of Athens and the island of Cephallonia. The sovereign rights of Venice were ignored; and the Republic did not venture to complain.

Amongst his Greek subjects Geoffrey II was as well liked as his father had been. But beneath the surface things were changing. A generation of *gasmoules* was growing up, dissatisfied with the contempt with which they were treated by the ruling Franks. They began to infuse a spirit of unrest amongst their mothers' kin. But to all appearances the Frankish dominion was not to be dislodged.

Geoffrey II died suddenly in 1246, still in the prime of his life. In spite of the pious foundation by the Princess Agnes of Cistercian monasteries whose monks had to pray for her to have children, Geoffrey was childless. His heir was his brother William.

William of Villehardouin had been born in Greece, at Kalamata, probably in 1211. He was a handsome man, his good looks marred only by his over-prominent teeth. He had already proved himself to be a fine soldier, but as a diplomat he lacked his brother's wisdom. He had been reared by Greek nurses and attendants; and he spoke Greek almost as fluently as his native French. He regarded himself as wholly belonging to his natal country. Many of the original settlers, such as Otho I of La Roche, lord of Athens, had in old age gone back home to the West. To William, Achaea was his home; and, like all his family, he was happiest at La Crémonie.

William's first acts as prince were to ensure the security of this beloved corner of the principality. It irritated him that Monemvasia was still in Greek hands. The Monemvasiots were energetic pirates who preyed on his shipping; and their harbour would provide far too convenient a landing-place should the Greeks ever seek to reconquer the Peloponnese. He made careful preparations. All his vassals were told to send troops, while the Venetians, who also suffered from Monemvasiot piracy, sent four ships to blockade the rock. There was no attempt to storm the fortress; but the blockade was steadily tightened. For three years the Monemvasiots held out, imprisoned, as the Chronicle of the Morea puts it, 'like a nightingale in a cage'. At last all their supplies ran out. The great cisterns were empty, and they had even eaten all the cats and the mice. So they surrendered. They were given honourable terms. The three joint archons were allotted estates on the mainland; and the townsfolk were excused all military service, but if they performed naval service they were to be paid for it.

While Monemvasia was still under siege, William completed the subjugation of the lawless tribes that lived in the mountains surrounding the vale of Sparta. Fortresses were needed to keep them in order.

The Tzakones could be cowed by the garrison at Monemvasia, once it was captured, and the strengthening of the castle at Geraki. To cow the Maniots there was already the castle of Passava; but William constructed a fortress called Great Maina near to the tip of Cape Matapan. It must be said that the taming of the Maniots was not wholly successful. A Latin bishop for Maina was appointed; but after a few years of discomfort and terror he obtained permission to reside permanently in Italy.

The most troublesome of the tribes was that of the Slav Milengi, who lived in the almost inaccessible valleys of Taygetus, dangerously close to Lacedemonia itself. To awe them and to ensure the safety of his favourite palace, William decided to build a castle on one of the nearby foothills of Taygetus. His professional eye fell on a conical hill rising some two thousand feet out of the plain, about four miles south-west of the city. On the west and south, precipices separated it from the main Taygetus range. On the north and east, the slopes were steep and easy to defend. From the summit the view extended on one side all over the plain of the Eurotas; on the other it looked up two great gorges into the heart of the mountain range. The road from Kalamata over the Langada pass, the only track across the range that was suitable for cavalry, came out into the plain a little to the north and passed close beneath the hill. The hill was known as Myzithra, probably because it was thought to resemble a local cheese which was made in the form of a cone. The name was later shortened to Mistras or Mistra. It was uninhabited, but there was a little chapel on the summit, dedicated no doubt to the prophet Elijah, the patron saint of mountains.

The great castle that William erected on the top of the hill was completed in 1249. He was well satisfied with it. It was admirably placed for keeping watch on the movements of the Milengi, and it would provide protection for his palace at La Crémonie.

All would have been well for the Prince had he curbed his ambition. His first wife had been of half-Greek blood. She was the daughter of Narjaud of Toucy (who had been regent for a year for the youthful Emperor Baldwin II, with the title of Caesar), and of the daughter of the French-born Empress Agnes (widow of the Emperors Alexius II and Andronicus I Comnenus) and her lover, the Byzantine traitor Theodore Branas. The young bride died within a few months of her marriage. On his deathbed Geoffrey II had urged his brother to marry again, lest the family of Villehardouin should become extinct. Soon after his accession William married a lady of Lombard origin, Carintana dalle Carceri, heiress to a third part of the island of Euboea. It seems to have been a happy marriage, but childless. On her death in 1255 William claimed her inheritance in Euboea. But she had uncles and cousins of the dalle Carceri clan who felt their rights to be stronger than those of her childless widower. They appealed for aid to the Venetians, who were glad for a chance to curb the power of a prince who had always disregarded their suzerainty. When William summoned his vassals to join him in an attack on Euboea, many of them ignored the summons. At their head was Guy of La Roche, lord of Athens, who owed allegiance as lord of Corinth and Argos and who had indeed recognized Geoffrey II as his general overlord. Guy was joined by his brother William, who was lord of Veligosti through marriage with its heiress, and, more seriously, by his son-in-law Geoffrey of Bruyères, lord of Karytaina, who was not only held to be the most brilliant soldier in the principality but was also Prince William's heir, being the son of his only sister. The war in Euboea dragged on until the army of Achaea was severely defeated by the Venetians in 1257 and the Prince had to retire back to the Peloponnese. But he was determined to punish his disloyal vassals, and in 1258 he marched on Thebes, where they had taken refuge. He met the Athenian army at Karydi, on the road from Megara to Thebes. The rebels were routed with heavy losses and fled back to Thebes. Prince William only consented not to storm and sack the town when its archbishop undertook to see that Guy and the other culprits came to Achaea to receive from the High Court whatever sentence it chose to give them. In the autumn of 1258 the High Court met at Nikli. Somewhat to their Prince's disappointment, the barons of Achaea declared that they were unable to pass any sentence on Guy, as he was the sovereign lord of Athens and therefore not one of their peers, even though he held Corinth under the Prince of Achaea. They recommended that the case be referred to the wisest monarch of the day, King Louis IX of France. Many of them had met the King, as Prince William had gone with a company of knights to pay his respects to him in Cyprus, when Louis was on his way to his Egyptian Crusade; and the disasters of that Crusade had not shaken their faith in his ability. Moreover, the Prince and most of his barons, being of French origin, felt that whomsoever they might nominally accept as suzerain, the King of France was their ultimate overlord. Guy of Athens was therefore ordered to go to France and receive his sentence from the King in person. It was more difficult for the Prince to forgive his nephew, Geoffrey of Bruyères. But when Geoffrey was brought before him with a halter round his neck and all the barons begged that he might be pardoned, William relented. Geoffrey was freed and his lands were returned to him, but as a personal gift from the Prince, without the feudal rights of a barony. Guy's brother, William of Veligosti, was also forgiven and his lands restored to him.

Prince William had been angered by his failure to obtain Euboea. After returning there in 1258 and defeating the Venetians a little inconclusively, he set out along a diplomatic path which he hoped would lead him to the dominant position in northern as well as southern Greece. The international situation in the Levant had changed greatly since his father's day. The Latin Empire of Constantinople was far gone in decay. The Emperor Baldwin II owned little outside of his own portion of the capital city and spent most of his time travelling round the courts of Europe begging for alms from his fellow-sovereigns. The Venetians were beginning to wonder whether it would be worth while to spend any effort on the retention of their portion of Constantinople. The Montferrat kingdom of Thessalonica had disappeared long since. In 1224 its capital had been captured by one of the Angelus princes of Epirus. William of Achaea, ruler of the Peloponnese and suzerain now of much of northern Greece, was the greatest Frankish potentate in the Christian East. His chief rival for power was the Byzantine Empire in exile, based on Nicaea. Its able emperor, John Vatatzes, who died in 1254, had in a reign of thirty-two years stripped Baldwin II of his Asiatic possessions, and then of his possessions in Thrace. He had advanced into Macedonia and in 1246 he captured Thessalonica from the Angeli. But his attempt to capture Constantinople in 1236 had been thwarted by the intervention of Geoffrey II of Achaea; and he had died leaving an empire surrounded by potential enemies, Turks on the east, Bulgarians on the north, Venetians in the centre, and very real enemies in the Prince of Achaea and the Angeli of Epirus.

The ruler of Epirus was now the Despot Michael II, an ambitious bastard who had come into power in about 1230. He was eager to recover his cousins' heritage of Thessalonica and he dreamed of marching eastward and capturing Constantinople itself before the Nicaeans could intervene. But first he must oust them from Macedonia.

Across the Adriatic there was another potentate ready to intervene in Greek lands. The great Emperor Frederick II had cultivated the friendship of John Vatatzes, both of them being the victims of papal hatred. But his bastard son, Manfred, who had inherited his Italian dominions, changed his policy. He tried to neutralize papal enmity by becoming the champion of the Popes' favourite client, Baldwin II. He also had ambitions to extend his domains across the Adriatic.

Michael of Epirus was a clever diplomat; and amongst his assets were two lovely daughters. In 1258, hearing that Manfred had recently been widowed, he offered him the hand of the lovelier, Helena, with Corfu and three towns on the Albanian mainland as her dowry. At the same time the other daughter, Anna, was offered to William of Achaea, who also was now a widower. Her dowry was to be lands in Thessaly. Both offers were accepted; and the two sons-in-law promised help to Michael against the Nicaeans. The moment seemed opportune. John Vatatzes' son and successor, Theodore II, had died in 1268, leaving the throne to a child; and there were quarrels in Nicaea over the regency. The emergence as regent, and then as emperor, of an able but unscrupulous nobleman, Michael Palaeologus, was not to everyone's liking.

These political intrigues seemed remote from the vale of Sparta; but it was from their outcome that the destiny of Mistra was to be settled, on a battlefield in northern Macedonia.

Michael of Epirus collected his army in the early summer of 1259. Manfred sent four hundred of his finest German knights; and William of Achaea came in person, with all his lords and the feudal levies of the principality. A contingent of Vlachs was brought by Michael's son, John, who married the daughter of a Vlach lord. The opposing army was led by John Palaeologus, brother of the new emperor Michael. He was a good general who had already made a successful incursion into Epirus; and he was adept at the Byzantine art of creating dissension inside the enemy camp. His army consisted of Greek infantrymen and a number of mercenary troops, Turks, Serbs and Cuman light cavalry from the Steppes, as well as some German knights under the Duke of Carinthia. It was a smaller army than the allies', but it had the advantage of a single commander.

The armies met on the plain of Pelagonia, near Monastir. On the eve of the battle John Angelus complained to Prince William that one of the Frankish lords had insulted his wife. He received no redress and therefore decided to withdraw his Vlachs. He told his father, who thought that it would be prudent to follow his example. Next morning Prince William and his troops and Manfred's German knights found themselves fighting without their Epirote allies. They fought well, but they were now outnumbered and outmanoeuvred. Within a few hours they were routed, and their leaders slain or taken prisoner. Prince William attempted to flee in disguise. He was discovered hiding under a bale of straw in a barn, and he was recognized by his prominent teeth.

The Battle of Pelagonia ended the great ambitions of the Angeli of

Epirus. It humiliated Manfred and helped to bring on his downfall seven years later. But it was the Villehardouin principality of Achaea that suffered most. When the news reached the Peloponnese, Princess Anna took the advice of the few remaining barons and sent to the court of France to ask Guy of Athens to return to administer the principality. His treason against the Prince was forgiven. Guy, chastened by having lived for several months in the austere company of St Louis, who had given him the title of Duke of Athens, performed his task with competence and tact, till the Prince should return from captivity.

Meanwhile the Prince and his barons had been taken to the court of Michael Palaeologus at Nicaea. They were honourably treated, and William was well liked by the Emperor and his courtiers owing to his fluency in the Greek language. But they were closely confined. At first the Emperor's terms for the release of his prisoners were that the whole principality should be ceded to him. In compensation he would give the Prince and his chief barons money for them to acquire large estates in France. Prince William refused the suggestion, explaining that the principality was not his to give away. His father had conquered it only as the leader of a number of lords of equal rank, and he could not dispose of any of its territory without the consent of their heirs. It is doubtful whether Michael ever seriously considered the annexation of the whole Peloponnese; it would have given him far too many problems. In the meantime, with the Angeli humbled and the Prince of Achaea in his power, and with the Venetians countered by an alliance that he made with the Genoese, his troops were able in 1261 to capture Constantinople, the Latin Emperor fleeing before them. Prince William and his barons were taken to watch the ceremonial entry of the Byzantine Emperor into his historic capital.

From this position of strength Michael now offered less grandiose but subtler terms. After asking for Nauplia and Argos and being told that they were fiefs of the Duke of Athens and that William had no power over them, he promised William and all his barons their liberty on condition that he was given the three strongholds of Monemvasia, Maina and Mistra. Here there was no constitutional objection. All three lay in a province which William's father had conquered and retained as his personal domain. William himself had conquered Monemvasia and constructed the castles of Maina and Mistra. William accepted the terms, subject to the consent of the High Court of the principality. His nephew, Geoffrey of Bruyères, lord of Karytaina, was sent by the Emperor to bring the terms before the Princess and the High Court of the principality. The Court met at Nikli in the late summer of 1261. It was known as the Parliament of Ladies, for its members were all the wives of captured lords or widows of those that had fallen, apart from two aged men and Geoffrey of Bruyères and the Duke of Athens. Duke Guy was in a difficult position. It suited him well that Prince William should stay in captivity; and everyone knew it. But he seems genuinely to have feared the strategic consequences of the cession of the castles. He argued that the terms be refused. The Emperor would surely release the Prince if a large enough ransom were raised; and he would pledge his duchy for it. But Geoffrey of Bruyères pointed out that to ransom every single lord would be a slow and costly business. The terms guaranteed the release of all of them. The ladies, with the Princess who presided at their head, voted to have their husbands returned to them. Geoffrey was sent back with their acceptance, taking with him two noble young ladies who should be hostages.

In the late autumn William of Villehardouin returned to his principality, with his nobles, having sworn allegiance to the Emperor and having stood as godfather to one of his sons. He was soon followed by Imperial officials, to whom he handed over the three fortresses, according to his bond. The standard of the house of Palaeologus, the two-headed eagle, flew once again over Monemvasia, and it flew for the first time over Maina and over the hilltop castle of Mistra.

IV The Return of the Greeks

IT WAS in the spring of 1262 that Byzantine officials arrived to take over the castle of Mistra. Of the territory acquired by the Emperor in Greece it was at first the least regarded. Monemvasia was an important seaport and had been under Frankish rule for only thirteen years. The great fortress of Maina dominated the wild peninsula that ended in Cape Matapan; and the district known as Kisterna, on the western side of the peninsula, was included in the lands ceded to the Emperor. In lower Laconia there was the fortress and small town of Geraki, whose lord, John of Nivelet, agreed to hand it over also, probably in return for a large sum of money, as he was able to acquire instead large estates near Aigion, on the shores of the Gulf of Corinth. But Mistra was a solitary outpost in lands that the Franks controlled. They still occupied the city of Lacedemonia at its feet; and the Villehardouins had no intention of abandoning their palace there. It was to Monemvasia that the governor – the *Kephale*, or 'Head' – of the new province was sent.

Mistra, however, grew rapidly. The Greeks of Lacedemonia began to move from a city where they were treated as second-class citizens in order to live under a governor of their own race and their own religion. They began to build themselves houses and churches on the hillside below the castle. It was not entirely a suitable site for a town. The slopes were steep, and there was little level ground. But it had advantages. Water was plentiful, and the air was healthier than in the plain. The Orthodox Metropolitan of Lacedemonia, who had not been allowed by the Franks to reside in his see, came to live in Mistra; and soon his successors, in the good ecclesiastical tradition, were warring with the Metropolitans of Monemvasia over questions of precedence.

It was not to be expected that the Emperor would long remain content with the lands that had been ceded to him, nor that Prince William would reconcile himself to their loss. In the summer of 1262 the Prince ostentatiously paid a visit to his favourite residence of La

Crémonie, in full view of the Greek garrison of Mistra. He was not afraid of provoking a war; for the Pope had obligingly told him that an oath made to a schismatic monarch when he was his prisoner was not binding in the eyes of God. The commander at Mistra hastily sent a messenger to Monemvasia, to the newly appointed governor, Michael Cantacuzenus. He in his turn reported the news to Constantinople, and in the meantime he got into touch with the Milengi tribes of Taygetus. In return for certain autonomous rights and for tax concessions, they promised him their support; and henceforward, though they did not abandon their brigand habits, they remained basically loyal to the Imperial governor. Gradually, being Orthodox in religion, and disliking the Latins as much as did the Greeks, they began to be absorbed into the Orthodox population of the Peloponnese.

On hearing the news from Monemvasia, the Emperor sent his young brother, the Sebastocrator Constantine Palaeologus, with other high officers and a regiment of Turkish mercenaries, to the Peloponnese. Constantine hastened to Mistra, where he confirmed the governor's arrangements with the Milengi and induced many of them to join his army, which was further strengthened by a number of *gasmoules*, the Franco-Greek half-castes whom the Franks despised but whom the Byzantines, who were lacking in racial prejudice and were willing to welcome as equals anyone who accepted the Orthodox faith, regarded as fellow-citizens.

Prince William had left Lacedemonia before Constantine arrived at Mistra. The Byzantine army therefore laid siege to the city. Then, hearing that William had gone to Corinth to discuss affairs with the Duke of Athens, Constantine decided to make a bold dash across the peninsula and attack the Frankish capital at Andravida. He marched past Veligosti, which his troops sacked, and past the Latin shrine of Our Lady of Isova, which they desecrated. Soon the advance guard reached Prinitsa, not far from Olympia. But there it was defeated by the Frankish garrison of Andravida and troops from the neighbouring fiefs. It was now late in the season of 1263. So Constantine retired swiftly back to Mistra. In the meantime a contingent of his army had penetrated northward to Kalavryta, where the local Greeks welcomed them and ejected the garrison of the local Frankish lord, Otho of Tournay, who was probably himself with the Prince at Corinth. Kalavryta was to remain for many decades a Greek enclave in Frankish territory.

The next spring the Sebastocrator set out again against the Franks. Luck was against him. While the main army laid siege to Nikli, the commander of the advance guard, the governor, Michael Cantacuzenus, was thrown from his horse, and before his followers could rescue him, Frankish soldiers came up and slew him. Worse followed. The money provided by the Emperor to pay the Turkish mercenaries had run out; and the Sebastocrator would not allow them to recoup themselves by looting the Greek villages. Claiming that six months' pay was due to them, they offered their services to Prince William, who gladly accepted them. About the same time the Sebastocrator was summoned back to Constantinople. He left the command in the Peloponnese to two generals, Philes and Macrenos. Hearing that the main Frankish army, swelled now by the Turks and under the command of Anselin of Toucy, was marching up the great pass of Makryplagi, which leads into central Arcadia, they planned an ambush. At first they were successful, and the Franks wavered. But then the Turks discovered a path that enabled them to attack the Greeks in the rear. The Greeks, who in fact were mainly Slavs and *gasmoules*, were surrounded. Most of them perished. A few managed to escape over the mountains, hotly pursued. The two commanders were discovered by the Turks sheltering in a grotto at Gardiki. They were brought before the Prince, who imprisoned them in the castle of Chlemoutsi. Philes died there. Macrenos was soon sent back to Constantinople in exchange for Anselin's brother, whom the Emperor held as prisoner. Soon after his return he was accused of treason by his mother-in-law, the Emperor's sister Eulogia, who suspected him of wishing to repudiate his wife and of having made plans to marry a princess of the rival Lascarid dynasty, who was the widow of the Frankish lord of Veligosti.

After their victory the Franks marched on Mistra. Though its garrison was depleted, its walls were still strong; and their attempts to storm them failed. Prince William came again to take up residence in his palace at Lacedemonia but it was no longer as pleasant as it had been. The town was deserted; for the Greek citizens had all moved to Mistra. William summoned Franks to come and take over the empty houses. But, after the wars, the Frankish population was too small for there to be colonists to spare. It was not long before William left his beloved La Crémonie never to return.

The result of the fighting was that, while the efforts of the Greeks to conquer the Peloponnese had come to nothing, they could not be dislodged from the fortresses that they had acquired. Meanwhile, Lacedemonia, the ancient Sparta, had come to the end of its history, not to rise again till the nineteenth century. Life in the vale of Sparta for nearly seven centuries to come was to find its centre at Mistra.

Both sides were ready for a truce. Prince William was worried about the future of his house; for he had no son, only two daughters. It was with some interest that he received a suggestion from the Emperor Michael that Michael's son, the co-Emperor Andronicus, should marry William's elder daughter, Isabella, and that the young couple should jointly inherit the Principality of Achaea. Such a marriage might well have brought peace to the peninsula, but it would have raised many problems, constitutional and religious; and, whatever the Prince may have thought of it, the barons of his High Court, suspecting that their feudal rights might be in jeopardy, insisted that the proposal be rejected. So the fighting went on, with desultory skirmishing along the borderlands.

In February 1266, Manfred of Hohenstaufen, King of Sicily, was defeated and killed at Benevento by the army of Charles, Count of Anjou, to whom the papacy had allotted the Sicilian kingdom, in order to be rid of the hated Hohenstaufen. Charles was the youngest brother of St Louis, King of France. He was a man of inordinate ambition, with none of the Saint's more amiable qualities. To the Europeans of the West, the loss of Constantinople to the Greeks had come as a humiliating shock. Charles saw himself as the protagonist in the restoration of the Latin Empire. The Emperor Baldwin II was wandering through Italy in impoverished exile. Manfred had been kind to him, but now he had to seek charity from Manfred's conqueror. At a treaty signed in May 1267, before Pope Clement IV in the papal palace at Viterbo, Baldwin ceded to King Charles all his suzerain rights over the Greek peninsula and the islands of the Ionian and Aegean Seas, retaining only his rights to the islands off the Anatolian coast, Lesbos, Chios, Samos and Cos, and Constantinople itself, all of which were in other hands. The treaty was to be cemented by the marriage of Baldwin's only son, Philip, with Charles's daughter Beatrice. The Prince of Achaea, whose interests were involved, sent as his representative his chancellor, Leonard of Veroli, who gave a pledge to support the treaty in the Prince's name. William·and his barons were delighted to accept King Charles as their overlord, in place of the futile Baldwin II, the more so as the Emperor Michael had just concluded a treaty with the Venetians which would greatly strengthen his hand in Greece. When, in the following year, young Conradin of Hohenstaufen led an army into southern Italy in a vain attempt to recover his inheritance, the Prince of Achaea crossed to Italy with many of his best knights to aid King Charles and to contribute to his victory at Tagliacozzo. Before he left Greece he had concluded a year's truce with the Byzantine governor; he felt that he could therefore spend several months at Charles's court. While he was there he and his suzerain planned the future of Achaea. Isabella, the Prince's elder daughter, was to marry King Charles's second son, Philip. The terms of the marriage contract were distinctly favourable to King Charles. If the young Prince were to die without issue the principality was to pass to the head of his family, not to any second husband of the legitimate heiress, nor, if she died too, to her sister. The arrangement was against feudal customary law; and the Prince was not altogether happy about it. He was believed to have made a will before his death in which his younger daughter Margaret was reinstated in the succession. But for the moment the friendship of King Charles was very valuable to him. Charles showered him with gifts and was always ready to send supplies of corn across the sea whenever the principality, ravaged by the wars, was in danger of famine. He could also provide the manpower that William now badly needed to hold the Greeks at bay.

Little is known about the wars of the next few years. In 1272 one of the Emperor's nephews arrived at Monemvasia with an army of Greeks and mercenaries, with which he was able to raid far into Frankish territory, but, it seems, without capturing any important castles. Two years later the Prince and his barons, with reinforcements sent by King Charles, organized a counter-raid and penetrated down the east coast of the Byzantine province as far as the outskirts of Monemvasia, but they did not venture to cross the forest-covered mountains into the vale of Sparta. By now the whole vale was in Greek hands. The Franks had all gone away; but their blood was still to be found there, in the *gasmoules* who came in to take service under the Imperial governor, though it seems that most of the *gasmoules* were settled round Monemvasia. Many of them enlisted in the Imperial navy.

To King Charles, control of the Peloponnese was important as part of his design to reconquer Constantinople for the West. But so long as the Greeks were contained in their corner he would not bother to oust them. The whole province would fall to him once he possessed Constantinople. The threat to his capital alarmed the Emperor, who had troubles on all his frontiers. In consequence, he had for some years been negotiating with the papacy, offering as a bait the submission of the Church of Constantinople to the Bishop of Rome. King Charles had won his kingdom as a papal nominee. It was therefore the Pope alone who could restrain his further ambitions. The negotiations dragged on inconclusively until the accession of Gregory X to the papacy in 1271. Gregory earnestly wished to drive the infidel from the

Holy Land; and the union of the Churches would be of great help to his scheme. He longed for King Charles to direct his efforts against the Muslims, and, if the schism were ended, he would certainly forbid him to attack Constantinople. Michael was not a pious man. He knew that the union, which he was quite ready to accept, would infuriate most of his clergy. But he was anyhow on bad terms with most of them, as they could not forgive him for breaking the oath that he had sworn to do no harm to the young Emperor whose throne he had usurped, and whom he imprisoned and blinded. But amongst his officials there were men of distinction and honour who were eager to end the schism, and others who disliked the thought of submission to Rome but would accept it if the interests of the State demanded it. So when Pope Gregory summonded a great Council to meet at Lyons in 1274, the Emperor was ready to send a delegation which was empowered in his name to bring the Church of Constantinople under the authority of Rome.

The union proclaimed at Lyons produced the political result that the Emperor desired. Charles of Anjou was obliged to give up, at least for a time, his preparations against Constantinople. But the lull was short-lived. It was easier for the Emperor to promise union than to persuade his people to comply. There was bitter opposition to it in Constantinople, led by the Emperor's own sister, Eulogia. Religious centres such as the communities on Mount Athos were particularly vociferous in their horror. No evidence has survived of the reaction in the Peloponnese; but it is difficult to believe that the local Orthodox, clergy and laity alike, who had suffered under the domination of the Latin Church, would have welcomed its return. The Emperor did his best to enforce his will, soon imprisoning and penalizing his chief opponents; but his decrees proclaiming the Union were disregarded. Priests who subscribed to it were deserted by their congregations. Papal agents in Constantinople reported to Rome that the Emperor was failing to carry his people with him. The papacy began to feel that it had been cheated.

It was during the lull that William of Villehardouin, Prince of Achaea, died, on May Day 1278. He had reigned for thirty-two years, popular with his subjects and admired even by his enemies. But the brilliance of his earlier years had not been sustained. He had lived to see his country worn out and impoverished by war and his loveliest province, with his favourite palace, lost for ever to the Greeks. He died, too, knowing that he had signed away his daughter's inheritance. Her husband Philip, King Charles's son, had died just over a year previously, leaving no children; and by the terms of the Treaty of

Viterbo the principality now passed into Charles's rapacious hands. Charles at once sent a bailli from Naples to take over the administration, Galeran of Ivry, who held the post for two years, to be succeeded by Philip of Lagonessa, who was also recalled after two years. His successor, Guy of La Trémouille, governed the province for three years.

In the meantime the papacy had grown exasperated by the Emperor's inability to implement the Union of Lyons. Gregory X had died in 1276. His three immediate successors each reigned for only a few months. Nicholas III, who ruled from 1277 to 1280, wrote sharply to Michael demanding more positive results. But Nicholas was a tactful diplomat. Moreover, he hated King Charles; and this hatred, so it was believed, by Dante amongst others, was fanned by gifts of Byzantine gold. His successor, however, was a Frenchman, Martin IV, who was an old friend of King Charles. In November 1281, he issued a Bill denouncing the Emperor as a perfidious heretic; and he gave his blessing to the expedition that King Charles now planned to launch against Constantinople, to put the titular Emperor Philip, Baldwin II's son and Charles's son-in-law, upon the Imperial throne, which Charles would then control. A great armada with a mighty army on board was assembling at Messina, ready to sail to the East in April 1282, as soon as the winter storms were over.

The Emperor Michael, with foes on all his frontiers and few friends amongst his own subjects, was close to despair. If this formidable expedition forced its way to the Bosphorus, could he hold his capital? He had an efficient fleet and a brilliant admiral, Licario, a man from Euboea of Lombard origin. But the fleet was small; it would be overpowered. At Mistra, when news came that the armada was to sail from Messina in the first week of April, the anxiety must have been as great as in Constantinople. If Constantinople fell once again to the Franks, the Greek province in the Peloponnese would have little chance of survival.

Deliverance came just in time. Of all King Charles's possessions it was the province of Sicily that most resented his rule. He took his title from the island, but he governed it from Naples and took little interest in its welfare. He distrusted and despised the Sicilians, allowing them no part in their administration, which was run by high officials of French origin, with Italians from the mainland working under them; and French troops garrisoned the island, treating the native inhabitants with a callous contempt. It was Sicily therefore which was chosen to be the base for a great conspiracy. The leading conspirator was an eminent doctor from Salerno, John of Procida, who as a young man had been the personal physician of the Western Emperor, Frederick II, and who had for a time served as King Manfred's chancellor. He now lived at the Court of Aragon, whose Queen was Manfred's daughter and, in John's eyes, heiress to his throne. He was determined somehow to ruin King Charles, whom he hated. Later legend told of him crossing the length of Europe in disguise: which is unlikely, as he was an old man whose official duties kept him in Aragon. But he had agents who passed between the courts of Constantinople and Aragon, the palaces of the Ghibelline lords of northern Italy, and towns and villages of Sicily itself; and the money for it all came from the treasury of the Emperor Michael. The power trail was laid. The spark was lit by a riot outside the Church of the Holy Spirit in Palermo on Easter Monday, 30 March 1282, when the bells were tolling for Vespers and the crowd waiting to enter the church was joined by a group of drunken French soldiers, one of whom insulted a Sicilian maiden. Her betrothed struck back at the Frenchman; and soon the whole crowd had joined in to slaughter his comrades. The rioters then rushed through the streets, calling fellow-citizens to come out with them, massacring every Frenchman that they saw and invading the houses and barracks where they were lodged. From Palermo the massacres spread all over the island. Soon every Frenchman in Sicily was dead or a fugitive, except only in Messina where King Charles's fleet was assembled, to sail in a few days' time against Constantinople.

The Sicilian Vespers, this massacre in a distant island, saved Mistra for the Greeks. Had Constantinople fallen to Charles's great armada, the Greek province in the Peloponnese could not have survived. But, with the island in flames, the fleet could not set out for the East; and soon Charles was involved in a bitter war against Aragon. All his schemes for a Mediterranean empire had to be abandoned for ever.

It was the Battle of Pelagonia, away in Macedonia, in 1259, that had given Mistra to the Greeks. It was the massacre of the Sicilian Vespers, away in Palermo, that ensured that they remained there. King Charles kept control of what remained of the the Villehardouin principality of Achaea, but he could not afford the troops now for any attempt to recover its lost lands. His instructions to his bailli, Guy of La Trémouille, in 1283, are concerned with the prevention of mercenary troops whom Guy had hired from going over to the Greeks or with organizing an exchange of prisoners so that various eminent local lords might be released. When Charles died in 1285, with his son and heir, Charles II, a captive in Aragonese hands, the government at Naples appointed two neighbouring magnates to be successively bailli, Guy de la Roche of Athens and Nicholas II of Saint-Omer of

Thebes. In 1289 Charles II, who had been freed in 1285, reversed his father's policy and allowed Isabella of Villehardouin, William's daughter, to enjoy her lawful inheritance. She had just been remarried, to a Belgian prince, Florent of Hainault, who took over the administration of the principality. Florent was an efficient ruler. He hastened to make peace with the Greeks of Mistra; and, though he had trouble with some of his Greek subjects and with raids from the Taygetus Slavs, the peace was maintained till he died in 1297. Isabella then carried on the government herself till 1301, when she married once again. Her new husband, Philip of Savoy, was about half her age, bellicose, avaricious and incompetent. After three disastrous years he retired to his lands in Italy and she to her dower-lands in Hainault. In 1307 they were deposed by their suzerain, Charles II of Naples, who gave the principality to his favourite son, Philip of Taranto. He arrived determined to restore its ancient glory; and in 1309 he defeated the Greeks of Mistra in battle and captured two or three frontier castles. That was the limit of his success. He grew bored and retired to Naples. Under his baillis the Greeks had little difficulty in recovering the lost fortresses.

Isabella and Florent of Hainault had had a daughter, Matilda, who was now the Dowager Duchess of Athens. In 1313 Philip of Taranto decided to marry the titular Latin Empress of Constantinople, Catherine of Valois. She was already betrothed to the Duke of Burgundy, so to console the Burgundian house for the breaking of the engagement, Philip arranged for Matilda of Hainault to marry the Duke's brother, Louis; and he bestowed on them the principality. Their reign was brief and troubled, first by the claims of Matilda's aunt, Margaret of Villehardouin, and then by her widowed son-in-law, Ferdinand of Majorca, in the name of his infant son James. Margaret was imprisoned by her own barons, who disliked her marrying her daughter to a Catalan prince; but Ferdinand, who had established himself at Chlemoutsi, was more dangerous. Eventually he was defeated and slain at a battle near Manolada in Elis in the summer of 1316. Louis of Burgundy had been wise enough to make friends with the Greeks of Mistra; and Greek soldiers had fought for him at the battle of Manolada. Had he lived he might have brought peace and prosperity to the Peloponnese. But within a month of his victory he was dead, poisoned, it was said, by the Count of Cephallonia.

Louis of Burgundy was the last Frankish prince of Achaea to have a sense of statesmanship. His widow Matilda was deposed for refusing to consummate a marriage ordered by the King of Naples to his brother, John, Count of Gravina, as she had secretly married a Burgundian knight. John, when Prince, organized a great expedition against Mistra in 1325; but it came to nothing. In 1333 he retired to Italy, handing over his claims to his nephew, Robert of Taranto: whose mother, the titular Latin Empress, Catherine of Valois, came herself to the peninsula and from 1338 to 1341 provided the principality with a fairly efficient administration, thanks chiefly to her lover, the Florentine banker Niccolò Acciajuoli. But when they both returned to Italy it soon fell into chaos. The Angevin heirs quarrelled amongst themselves. The King of Majorca, the son of the Infant Ferdinand, claimed to be prince: which gave the Catalan Company, now established in Athens, the chance to intervene. Great feudatories such as Nerio Acciajuoli, who had taken over the estates accumulated by Niccolò, his cousin and adopted father, or the Bishop of Patras, ignored the authority of any prince. The Hospitallers, to whom Queen Joanna I of Naples leased the principality in 1376, never achieved control of it. When the last Angevin representative, James of Les Baux, died in 1283, there were five claimants to the title of prince; but the power was in the hands of the Navarrese Company, which had come to Greece a few years previously, in the hope of imitating the success of the Catalan Company. In 1396 the Commander of the Company, Peter of San Superan, proclaimed himself Prince. On his death in 1402 his widow, Maria Zaccarione, of the Genoese family that now ruled Chios, was ousted by her nephew, Centurione Zaccaria, who was the last Latin to rule as Prince of Achaea. In the meantime Venice had strengthened her hold on Methone and Corone, and had acquired in 1388, by purchase from their heiress, control of the cities of Nauplia and Argos.

In such circumstances, the Greeks of Mistra no longer had anything to fear from the Franks, and they could set about the reconquest of the whole Peloponnese. It was slow work. The country was wild, the local lords lawless; and the Greek authorities had only small resources in troops. But there were now Latin lords who preferred to come under the rule of the Greeks rather than that of the feeble Latin princes and gradually to be absorbed into the Greek nobility. Mistra itself was now emerging as the capital city of a prosperous and growing dominion.

V The Despot Manuel

FOR SOME sixty years Monemvasia remained the headquarters of the *Kephale*, the governor of the Byzantine Peloponnese. It was an obvious choice. From there he could keep in regular contact by sea with Constantinople, while Mistra was still an outpost in territory as yet controlled by the Franks, and Maina was an isolated castle set in a wild peninsula. But as the province grew in size, Monemvasia, away in its south-eastern corner, was ill-placed to be its centre. Mistra was now far more suitable. With the Taygetus range to protect its rear and the rich vale of Sparta at its feet, it was becoming a secure and prosperous town to which Greeks from all over the Peloponnese were coming to settle. In 1270 the *Kephale* was still living at Monemvasia, but by 1289 he had moved to Mistra. The move was probably made after the death of William of Villehardouin in 1278, when there was no likelihood of the Franks returning to the vale of Sparta.

At first the *Kephale* was appointed for one year only. The first *Kephale* was a member of the family of Cantacuzene, which had owned lands in the Peloponnese before the Frankish conquest. He remained in the province after his term of office came to an end and was killed in the foray in the spring of 1264. His prowess as a soldier was admired by the Franks. It is uncertain whether any of the generals whose names are mentioned in the history of the next few years was a local governor or a soldier sent out to conduct a special campaign. In about 1285 the system of government was changed. It seemed wiser to the authorities in Constantinople to give the governor a longer period of office, with the higher title of *Epitropos*. This would make for greater continuity in the administration. Moreover, as piracy was growing in the Aegean Sea it might not be easy to send out a new governor and his staff every year to the Peloponnese. The first governor under the new arrangement was another member of the Cantacuzene family, perhaps a nephew, or, just possibly, a son of the gallant governor who had died in 1264. He was a very young man, aged only twenty-one. His first name is not known; but if the family followed the usual practice of calling the eldest grandson by the paternal grandfather's name (unless the maternal grandfather was much more distinguished), then we may assume that he was called Matthew. He must have shown great promise to have secured the appointment; and his administration seems to have justified the confidence that the Emperor Andronicus II placed in him. But after eight years in the province he suddenly died, still under thirty.

The next governor whose name is known to us was a man of high distinction, Andronicus Palaeologus Asen, whose father was an ex-king of Bulgaria and whose mother was a sister of the Emperor Andronicus II. He was already in office in the year 1315 and remained in Mistra until 1321. His government was marked by many successes against the Franks, from whom he captured the great castles of Akova and Karytaina, and so established Byzantine control over the central province of Arcadia. This hold was strengthened when Andronicus defeated a relieving Frankish army in front of the Arcadian castle of St George, slaying the commander of the Teutonic Knights and taking prisoner the Chief Constable, Bartolomeo Ghisi. The lesser Frankish lords accepted Greek domination and were confirmed in their possessions. Within a generation they began to adopt the Orthodox faith and to intermarry with their Orthodox fellow-citizens. Andronicus's last years in Greece seem to have been mainly occupied in warding off attacks from the Catalan Company, which now was in control of Athens. His departure was greatly regretted; but he wished to play his part in the political dramas that marked the declining years of his uncle, the Emperor Andronicus II.

It was at this point that Andronicus II offered the governorship to the most brilliant young man at the court, John Cantacuzenus. It was the natural choice; for John was the son – born just before or just after his father's death – of the young general who had governed the province early in the Emperor's reign, and he had recently married the daughter of Andronicus Asen. John refused the assignment, saying that his family had sad memories of the Peloponnese and his mother had told him that it would grieve her deeply were he to accept an appointment in a land that had caused his father's death. The excuse was certainly disingenuous. His mother, to whom he was devoted, was a lady of great energy and ambition and was not going to allow her son to be side-tracked into a distant province when so much was happening in Constantinople. But she did allow him to accept the post of governor of Thessaly, where he would have a large army and ample resources at his disposal. As it turned out, he never took up the appointment, owing to the intensification of the crisis in Constantinople.

In John's place, the governorship of the Peloponnese seems to have been given to a certain Andrew. All that we know of him is that he was appointed by 'the pious Emperor Andronicus' – the epithet fits Andronicus II better than Andronicus III, who was not very pious, but it was often given formally to emperors, regardless of their character – and that he was the father of a saint, Leontius of Achaea, who was noted for his good works later in the century. His period of office may have been short. In 1325 the military commander of the Greeks bore the title *Protokynegus*; whether he was governor is uncertain.

There followed a desolate period in the history of the Greek Peloponnese. The Catalan Company had been conducting raids into the peninsula since before the end of the thirteenth century. Indeed, in 1292 the Catalan admiral Roger de Lluria had captured and sacked the lower towns of Monemvasia and Maina, and had retired laden with booty and with prisoners whom he sold in the slave-markets in Sicily. Andronicus Asen had kept the Catalans in check during his governorship; after his departure the raids recommenced, mostly by land, but they never penetrated as far as the vale of Sparta. More formidable were raids by pirates sailing from the Turkish ports on the Aegean coast of Anatolia. These began to be serious in the 1320s. In 1332 Umur, Emir of Aydin, sacked the lower town of Monemvasia, capturing the local governor and his daughter, who were, however, rescued by the Venetian admiral Zeno before they could be sold as slaves. Two years later Umur landed troops in the Laconian Gulf and marched up the Eurotas valley as far as Mistra itself. But the strength of the city walls overawed him; and he retired after receiving a handsome present from the governor.

Disorders in the province were increased by the outbreak of civil war in Byzantium, after the death of Andronicus III in June 1341. Shortly before his death a delegation from several of the Frankish nobility arrived in Constantinople to inform John Cantacuzenus, then chief minister, that they wished to come under the rule of the governor of Mistra. But before he could take any action on their request he was at war with rival politicians who had won the support of the Empress-Mother, Anna of Savoy, governing in the name of the child-Emperor, John V. It was not until John Cantacuzenus entered Constantinople and took over the government as the Emperor John VI that he could pay attention to the Peloponnese. During the intervening years the governors of Mistra, none of whose names have survived, seem to have lost control of the various Greek and Latin lords in the countryside.

As emperor, John Cantacuzenus was concerned to restore order to the Peloponnese, for which he felt a family responsibility. Early in 1349 he appointed his younger son, Manuel, to whom he had recently given the title of Despot, to be governor of the province. Manuel was in his early twenties, a young man of remarkable energy and ability. It is unlikely that he was given any special viceregal powers on his appointment. But communications with Constantinople were often interrupted; and Manuel pursued his own policy without reference to the Imperial government. This, and his high rank as an emperor's son, gave a special prestige to the province; and Manuel clearly considered that he had been appointed for his lifetime. The province thus became an autonomous appanage. We can henceforward speak of the Despotate of the Peloponnese, or the Morea, though, in fact, neither Manuel nor any of his successors as Despot, even in their official documents and inscriptions, added a territorial designation to their title.

Manuel soon showed his quality. Shortly before leaving Constantinople he married a lady of Latin descent. She was the daughter of a Cypriot prince, Guy of Lusignan, who had spent much of his youth in Constantinople and had twice had a Byzantine bride. Her mother seems to have been the second wife, who was connected with the Palaeologan dynasty. Guy had eventually succeeded to the throne of Cilician Armenia, his mother being a princess of the Armenian Hethoumian dynasty. He was assassinated in 1344, two years after his accession. Manuel's wife bore several names. An inscription in Mistra calls her 'Zampea nte Lezinao', but a later one, at Longanikos in Laconia, calls her Maria, while she appears in Cypriot sources as Margaret. Perhaps in later life she was received into the Orthodox Church and was re-baptized Maria. But her sympathies seem to have been Latin; and she kept in touch with her Latin relatives in the Christian East.

It was probably due to her influence that Manuel, as ruler of the Greek Peloponnese, made it his policy to keep on friendly terms with the Latins in the peninsula. It was with the help of Latin lords that he cowed the disorderly Greek lords in the province into submission. In about 1358 he made an alliance with the Latin governor of Achaea and the Venetians against the Turks. The allies secured a victory off the coast of Megara, in which thirty-five Turkish ships were destroyed. The Turks, however, obtained the support of the Catalan Company, under their Captain, the younger Roger de Lluria. A second expedition was necessary to restrain them. During the next few years Turkish raids were less frequent. Manuel also intervened in the internal affairs of the Franks. When the prince, Robert of Taranto, died without issue in 1364, his widow, Marie of Bourbon, sought to secure the principality for her son by her first marriage, Hugh of Lusignan, Prince of Galilee, who had been passed over for the Cypriot throne and was seeking an alternative domain. Manuel, whose wife was Hugh's cousin, supported him against the more lawful candidate, Robert of Taranto. He did well from it all. When Hugh renounced his claims for a large sum of money, a good portion of it was given to Manuel, who had also acquired a few villages and forts in the course of the war. However, a few years later, in 1375, when Queen Joanna of Naples had taken over the principality, her bailli, Francis of Sanseverino, attacked and captured the town of Gardiki and laid siege to its great castle. Manuel brought an army to its rescue, and was severely defeated. But Sanseverino found the castle impregnable and soon gave up the siege.

In pursuit of his general policy Manuel was careful to keep on good terms with the Latin Church. We find him conducting a friendly correspondence with Pope Gregory XI, who seemed to have hopes of his conversion; and he smoothed out any signs of local friction between Orthodox and Latin hierarchs. This made it easier for Latin lords to accept Greek rule. The governor of Gardiki, Syryannis Gilopoulos, or Sir John, son of Giles, was certainly one of them. By the end of the fourteenth century many of the notable Greek families of the Peloponnese had names of Western origin, Phrangopoulos, or son of the Frank, Raoul, Phrantzes or Sphrantzes, derived from Francis, or Petrobua.

Internally Manuel had his difficulties. Soon after his arrival in the Peloponnese he decided that it was essential to build a small fleet and that the local lords should contribute towards the cost. A certain Lampoudius undertook to collect the money from them, but instead of carrying out his assignment he went round the countryside inciting them to revolt against the Despot. A group of rebels prepared to march on Mistra. But they were undisciplined and jealous of each other; and when they were faced by Manuel's army of only some three hundred men, the revolt collapsed.

More embarrassing were Manuel's difficulties with his family. In December 1354, John VI Cantacuzenus abdicated in favour of his son-in-law, John V Palaeologus, the legitimate emperor, and put on the habit of a monk. But John VI's elder son, Matthew, who had been crowned co-emperor, refused to work under John V. For some months he ruled independently at Adrianople. In the summer of 1355 John VI arranged peace terms between his son and his son-in-law, by which Matthew would take over the government of the Peloponnese and Manuel would be compensated by the government of the small island of Lemnos. Manuel was not consulted and would certainly not willingly have agreed to the terms. But, before they could be implemented, war broke out again between John V and Matthew, which resulted in Matthew's capture and imprisonment. When peace was eventually made in December 1357, and Matthew renounced the Imperial title but was given precedence next to the Emperor John V and his heir, no mention was made of the Peloponnese. But in the meantime John V had decided to replace Manuel by two of his cousins, the brothers Michael and Andrew Asen. They arrived in the Peloponnese in the latter half of 1355. The local Greek lords, still smarting under the fiasco of their attempted revolt under Lampoudius, hastened to welcome the new governors; and for a time Manuel's authority did not extend beyond the walls of Mistra. But the people in general supported Manuel. He also had the influential help of the Venetians, whom the Asen brothers had offended by raiding their lands in the Peloponnese and who made it clear to Constantinople that they would oppose the new regime. After a few months the Asens found that they were making no headway and retired to Constantinople. The Emperor John V was probably relieved. He confirmed Manuel's post.

In 1361 the two ex-emperors John VI and Matthew Cantacuzenus came to visit Manuel; and Matthew decided to settle in Mistra. As the elder son and a former emperor he expected Manuel to hand over the governorship to him. Manuel saw no reason for doing so. A compromise was arranged. Matthew was associated with Manuel in the government; but, in fact, Manuel remained in control. Matthew, though he made his home in Mistra, seems to have made occasional visits to Constantinople. His wife and children came to join him there, with the exception of his eldest daughter, who was a nun in Constantinople. The second daughter, Helena, was married in about 1366 to the Aragonese Count of Salona, in northern Greece. The youngest daughter, Maria, married a Byzantine nobleman with Cypriot connections and religious sympathies with Rome. There is some uncertainty about the parts played by Matthew's sons. It is probable that the elder, John, who had the title of Despot, took no part in public life but devoted himself to good works, while the younger, the Sebastocrator Demetrius, was more ambitious.

The arrangement made between Manuel and his brother worked out smoothly. Matthew, once he was assured of an honourable position, did not interfere in the government but devoted himself mainly to intellectual studies, writing works on philosophy and religion. Their father, the ex-Emperor John VI, paid occasional visits to Mistra, to assure himself that all was going well. It seems that the brothers' wives were equally friendly with each other. Matthew's wife, Irene Palaeologaena, was gentle and self-effacing. Isabella-Maria of Lusignan acted as the chief lady of the province. It was she who was hostess to her cousin, King Peter I of Cyprus, when he visited Mistra in 1371; and soon afterwards she went on a long visit to Cyprus. Her marriage to Manuel was childless. There was no rivalry between cousins of the next generation. Matthew and Manuel shared a taste for learning and the arts, and both were liked and admired by the eminent philosopher–historian, Nicephorus Gregoras, much as he disapproved of their father's theology.

Manuel died in 1380. He had been a firm but kindly ruler; and he was greatly mourned. He was the ablest and the most attractive of the Despots of the Peloponnese. His death put the government into the hands of his brother Matthew. But Matthew had long since lost any ambition for power. He was ready to accept any new arrangement that the Emperor John V might ordain. However, John V had other distractions at the moment. For the last four years he had been fighting against his eldest son, Andronicus IV, who for a time had usurped the throne and thrust him into prison with his loyal younger sons, Manuel and Theodore. He had escaped and recaptured Constantinople. But Andronicus still held as hostages his own mother, the Empress Helena, John V's wife and Matthew's sister, together with the old ex-Emperor John VI Cantacuzenus, his wife and his other daughters. It was well into 1381 before a family peace was patched up, largely through the influence of John VI. John V remained senior Emperor. Andronicus was given an appanage in Thrace, with the title of Emperor, and Manuel, also as Emperor, Thessalonica and what remained of Byzantine Macedonia. Theodore, with the title of Despot, was to go to the Peloponnese.

Immediately afterwards John Cantacuzenus travelled to Mistra to inform Matthew of the settlement. Till Theodore should arrive Matthew continued to govern the province, with his aged father acting as his chief adviser. It is to this period that a letter to him from the savant, Demetrius Cydones, can be dated, in which Matthew is called a modern Lycurgus, ruling Lacedaemon with justice and wisdom and profiting from the sage advice of his venerable father. Unfortunately, Matthew's son Demetrius, who had hoped to rule the province himself, rose in revolt, securing the support not only of the local Greek lords, who had always resented the government at Mistra, but also a number of Turkish pirates and raiders. When Theodore arrived in the Peloponnese in December 1382, most of the Byzantine province was in Demetrius's hands. Theodore could make little headway against him. But at the end of 1383 or the beginning of 1384 Demetrius died, and the revolt collapsed.

On Theodore's appearance at Mistra, both Matthew and his aged father retired from the court. John VI died a few months later, in a local monastery, on 15 June 1383. Nine days later, Matthew followed his father to the grave.

VI The Despot Theodore I

FEW DYNASTIES have been more gifted than that of the Palaeologi, who reigned over Byzantium for the last two centuries of its existence. Its princes and princesses were fame for their handsome looks. With hardly an exception they were highly cultured, deeply interested in learning and the arts and able to correspond with the leading savants of the time. All of them had a personal charm that won them devoted adherents. But, apart from the founder of the dynasty, Michael VIII, and the Emperor Manuel II, in so far as circumstances allowed him any scope, none of them was possessed of political judgment or foresight; and they quarrelled perpetually with each other. Sons would intrigue and even fight against fathers, brothers against brothers, regardless of the harm that might be done not only to the dynasty but also to the dwindling empire over which they precariously presided. Rivalries within the family were intensified in the fourteenth century by the growing system of appanages. In the old days the senior Emperor had been the Autocrator. His brothers and sons had to obey his supreme authority. But now Constantinople could no longer provide good government for its scattered provinces. Junior members of the family were allotted provinces which they could rule with almost complete autonomy. Consequently, if they were not struggling to obtain the Imperial throne itself, they struggled with each other to obtain the richest appanage. Meanwhile, the Turkish menace grew year by year. The Turks were established in Europe by the middle of the century. Well before its end they dominated the Balkan peninsula; and the provinces of Byzantium were isolated enclaves. Commerce was in the hands of the Venetians and the Genoese, whose passionate rivalry, while it might at times be politically convenient to their neighbours, damaged the prosperity of the whole Levant.

Theodore I Palaeologus was aged about thirty when he arrived at Mistra. He was the third son of John V and Helena Cantacuzene, John VI's daughter. In the war between his eldest brother Andronicus and

John V he had supported his father, perhaps less from filial love than from a fraternal affection, rare in his family, for his second brother, Manuel. During Andronicus's period of triumph he had shared his father's and Manuel's uncomfortable imprisonment in the Tower of Anemas in Constantinople. It must have been with relief that he left the turbulent capital for Mistra. Once there, he acted with complete disregard for the Imperial government, while his father, his brother Andronicus and Andronicus's son John VII continued to fight for power. It was only when his brother Manuel took over the Empire in 1391 that relations between Constantinople and Mistra became close again.

Theodore's first task after his arrival was to crush the revolt of the Greek lords, led by his cousin, Demetrius Cantacuzenus. The most formidable of these rebels were the members of the Mamonas family, who owned large estates round Monemvasia and much of the town itself. In 1384, partly because he despaired of reducing the rebels and partly because he was indebted politically, and probably financially, to the Venetian Republic, he wrote to the Venetian bailli at Constantinople offering to cede Monemvasia to Venice. The offer shocked most of Theodore's subjects; and Mamonas and his fellow-Monemvasiots refused to admit the Venetians. The offer had to be withdrawn. Fortunately for Theodore, the death of Demetrius Cantacuzenus, which followed soon afterwards, obliged the Mamonas family grudgingly and temporarily to submit to the government at Mistra.

While the Despot Manuel's policy had been to maintain peace as far as he could with his neighbours and to bring prosperity to his subjects, Theodore was a restless soldier and diplomat, determined to increase his dominions. It would have been difficult for him to act otherwise; for the remnant of the Frankish Principality of Achaea had been, since 1380, in the hands of the Navarrese Company, acting at first as the titular agents of James of Les Baux, its nominal prince, but later setting up their own leader as prince. Theodore was permanently at war with them. Officially he supported the rival claim to the princedom of the Count of Savoy, who happily had no intention of appearing personally in Greece. So the Despot was able to retain what conquests he made from the Navarrese. The Knights Hospitaller, to whom Queen Joanna of Naples had leased the principality for five years in 1377, made no attempt to renew the lease and had withdrawn. But Theodore regarded them as useful potential allies.

His chief ally was Nerio Acciajuoli, of the Florentine banking family. Nerio had taken over the vast Peloponnesian estates of his cousin Niccolò, which included the town and fortress of Corinth. In

1374 he had occupied Megara and in about 1383 the lower town of Athens, though the Acropolis did not fall into his power till 1388. In 1385 Theodore married Nerio's elder daughter Bartolomea, who was not only considered to be the loveliest woman of her time, but also, as Nerio had no legitimate son, was likely to be a great heiress. Indeed, Nerio promised that on his death she would inherit Corinth. Little is known of the Despoena Bartolomea, apart from her beauty. Her marriage was childless but seems to have been happy, though Theodore had at least one bastard child. She gave loyal support to her husband.

The alliance with Nerio was very useful to Theodore, especially in his wars against the Navarrese. Both, too, were soon on bad terms with the Venetians. This led them to plan an ambitious *coup*. In 1388 the Venetian husband of Maria of Enghien, the heiress of Argos and Nauplia, suddenly died, and the widow, feeling defenceless, agreed to sell her possessions for a large capital sum and an annuity to the Venetian government. Theodore and Nerio hastened to invade the territory before the Venetian governor could arrive. Theodore occupied Argos, with its citadel of Larissa, high above the town, while Nerio occupied Nauplia, with its twin castles, the 'Greek' and the 'Frankish'. When the Venetians arrived they were able to recapture Nauplia but could not dislodge the Despot's troops from Argos. Fortunately for Venice, the Navarrese Company, its ally for the time being, disregarding a safe conduct given to Nerio when he came in September 1389 to negotiate with its Commander, took him prisoner and refused to let him go until Argos should be handed over to Venice. Theodore did not see why he should be penalized by his father-in-law's folly in trusting the Navarrese Company's sense of honour and held on to Argos. In 1391 Nerio was released, on promising to let the Venetians hold his city of Megara till they should have Argos. Theodore remained obdurate. Relations between him and Nerio grew chilly, though Nerio still wanted his help against the Navarrese, whose treachery he could not forgive. A treaty was signed at last in May 1394, between Theodore and the Venetians, in which he gave up Argos and the neighbouring territory, demanding only that the Greeks who wished to move into his lands should be allowed to do so with all their movable goods and that the fiefs that he had allotted to Greeks should not be confiscated. A further, ominous, demand was that should he be forced to leave his lands, Venice would provide him and his family a safe refuge.

The reason for Theodore's abandonment of Argos was the approach of an enemy far more dangerous than the Venetians. After their great victory over the Serbs at Kossovo in 1389 the Ottoman Turks turned their attention to the Greek peninsula. During the next two years, Evrenos Bey, Sultan Bayazet's leading general, occupied Thessaly, which was given to him as a fief. He was now preparing to advance further into Greece. The Navarrese Company decided that the Turks would be useful friends. Early in 1394 the Commander, Peter of San Superan, made his way to the Sultan's court to ask for aid. There he met the lord of Monemvasia, Mamonas, who had risen once more against the Despot and who, after toying with the idea of offering his city to the Venetians, was now offering it to the Turks. In April, Sultan Bayazet was in Macedonia. After occupying Thessalonica he summoned the Emperor Manuel and the Despot Theodore to wait upon him at Serres. The two brothers were treated with studied discourtesy. Theodore was told to reinstate Mamonas and, at the request of the Navarrese, to yield up Argos. The Sultan's threats made it clear that he intended before long to eliminate both of the brothers.

In such circumstances Theodore could not afford to alienate the Venetians. Argos was ceded; and the Venetians secured various economic concessions, the most curious of which was to forbid the Despot from continuing to mint imitation Venetian ducats, which seem to have formed the chief currency in his dominions, commanding more respect than honest Byzantine coins would have done. The concessions did him little political good. Venice was desperately anxious not to provoke the Turks into open hostility.

Soon afterwards, in September, Nerio died at Athens. In his will he left the city to the Church of the Holy Virgin there, the building that we call the Parthenon. To his illegitimate son Antonio he bequeathed the city of Thebes, over which his control was tenuous. All his other possessions, including Corinth and his Peloponnesian estates, were allotted to his younger daughter, Francesca, the wife of Carlo Tocco, Duke of Cephallonia and Leucas, and now the most powerful Latin prince in Greece. To his elder daughter, Bartolomea, the wife of the Despot, he left only the sum of 9,700 ducats, a sum which her husband had borrowed from him to pay off a debt to the Venetians. Theodore and Bartolomea, who had been promised when they married that they would have the reversion of Corinth, were furious, and determined to capture their expected inheritance by force of arms.

The war had to be delayed for a few months. Theodore had, it seems, left the Ottoman camp at Serres without the Sultan's permission and had to be punished. In the spring of 1395 a Turkish army marched across the Isthmus of Corinth and ravaged Arcadia, returning laden with booty. Mistra and the vale of Sparta had been spared for the moment. The Turks were now distracted by the Crusade planned by King Sigismund of Hungary. Theodore could set out to conquer Corinth, adding to his army such Turkish soldiers as were left in southern Greece and had not been hired by the Navarrese. He and his army were defeated outside Corinth by the allies of Carlo Tocco; but further south, near Leontarion, his general, Demetrius Raoul, defeated the Navarrese and captured their Commander, Peter of San Superan. Without Navarrese help it was impossible to dislodge Theodore's troops from the neighbourhood of the Isthmus. An unfortunate Italian notary on his way home from Athens describes the appalling state of the countryside in the autumn of 1395. He found the gates of Megara closed against all travellers lest they should be agents of the Despot. The road to Corinth was infested by Turkish soldiers who lived as brigands. Near the Isthmus he managed to avoid an ambush laid by the Despoena Bartolomea, who hoped to waylay her hated sister journeying from Megara to take a boat from Corinth on her way to Cephallonia.

By the end of 1395 Carlo Tocco decided that Corinth was not worth so much trouble and ceded it, with the citadel of Acrocorinth, to the Despot. About the same time, in December 1395, Theodore released San Superan from captivity, in return for the sum of fifty thousand pieces of gold, paid by the Venetians, who were anxious to preserve the Navarrese power as a counter-balance to the Greeks and who knew that Theodore could not afford to refuse such an addition to his depleted treasury.

In September 1396, Sultan Bayazet overwhelmed King Sigismund and his Crusaders at the battle of Nicopolis and was free to turn his attention once more to Greece. Theodore pleaded with the Venetians to join him in the defence of the Peloponnese. His ambassador, Demetrius Sophianus, was empowered to offer them the city of Corinth in return for military and naval help. It was in vain. The Senate was determined not to risk an open breach with the Sultan. The ambassador was still in Venice when two great Turkish armies marched to the Isthmus of Corinth. Theodore, when at last he had taken possession of Corinth, had made it his first task to restore the Hexamilion, the great wall that ran across the Isthmus. But it could not stand up to the attack of an army of fifty thousand men.

The Venetians were punished for their cowardice. One Turkish army, led by Yakub Pasha, moved quickly down to their city of Argos. While the Venetian governor cowered in the citadel of Larissa, the Argive citizens bravely defended their walls. But after a few days the Turks broke through the defences. The whole city was sacked. Many thousands of the people were massacred; and it was said that thirty thousand miserable captives trailed back northward with Yakub Pasha's troops, to be sold as slaves in Anatolia.

The second army, under Evrenos Bey, turned into Arcadia. Theodore attempted to intercept it at Leontarion but was severely defeated; and Evrenos Bey swept on as far as the walls of the Venetian fortresses of Corone and Methone, ravaging as he went, and destroying the farms and orchards owned by the Venetian colonists. But as yet the Turks did not leave any garrisons behind them. They retired with their booty back to Thessaly.

Once again the vale of Sparta had been untouched. But Theodore had little hope for the future. He was now a sick man. His wife seems to have died about this time, and he had no children apart from a bastard daughter; she, it seems, had been sent to be brought up in Constantinople. In his despair, Theodore once again sent his ambassador to Venice. But a Venetian embassy was at the Sultan's court, planning a treaty of non-aggression, which was signed in July 1399. Once again the Senate was not to be tempted by the offer of Corinth. At this juncture the Grand Master of the Knights Hospitaller sent an embassy from his headquarters at Rhodes to Mistra, to suggest that the Despot should sell Corinth to the Order. Theodore hesitated. The Emperor Manuel had recently passed through the Peloponnese on his way to plead for help from the courts of the West. He had left Constantinople in the hands of his nephew, John VII, but not trusting him greatly he brought his wife, the Empress Helena, and their two sons to Mistra to leave them in his brother's care. Theodore seems to have consulted his sister-in-law, who advised him to accept the offer; and Manuel, when he learnt of it, also gave his approval. In the spring of 1400 Corinth passed into the hands of the Order.

Once established in Corinth, the Order wished to enlarge its Peloponnesian possessions. Later that spring it sent an embassy to Mistra to suggest that the Despot should sell it Kalavryta, in the north of the peninsula, and Mistra itself, with the assumption that it would take over the whole of Arcadia and the vale of Sparta. The Despot himself was to retire to Monemvasia. Theodore could not consult the Emperor, who was far away in the West; and the Empress seems to have returned to Constantinople. In his melancholy despair he agreed to the bargain. At the end of May the Knights entered Kalavryta, to be received with sullen resentment by its inhabitants. At Mistra the population rose in riot. The Knights' delegates who had come to arrange for the take-over would have been lynched had the Metropolitan not given them his protection and soothed the rioters. Theodore, who was on his way to Monemvasia, was not readmitted into Mistra until he promised to repudiate the transaction: while Sultan Bayazet hastened to inform Theodore that if he wished to enjoy the Sultan's friendship he must eject the Knights from the peninsula.

The year 1401 was spent in acrimonious negotiations between the Knights and Theodore, whom they considered had let them down. Then suddenly the situation changed. The Sultan was threatened from the east by the great Tartar conqueror, Timur, or Tamurlane. In the summer of 1402, at the battle of Ankara, Bayazet was routed and himself taken prisoner by Timur. With the Sultan in captivity and his sons quarrelling over the inheritance, and with its main army annihilated, it seemed that the Ottoman Empire was about to collapse.

In the long run the Ottoman disaster at Ankara did nothing to help the Greeks. Timur had no intention of invading the Turkish provinces in Europe; and when he died in 1405 his whole empire began to disintegrate. In the meantime more and more Turks, seeking to avoid Tartar domination, crossed the Straits to settle in Europe. It would be hard to prevent their further expansion there. But the immediate effect was heartening. The Greeks were able to recover Thessalonica as well as some coastal towns in Thrace; and pressure on the Greek peninsula was lessened. Theodore began to regret his bargain with the Knights Hospitaller. He sought the diplomatic assistance of his brother, the Emperor, who hurried back from the West on the news of the Sultan's defeat. In 1404, under Manuel's guidance, a new treaty was signed. Since 1393 the Turks had held the great fortress of Salona, not far from the northern coast of the Gulf of Corinth, whose last Christian owners had been the Dowager Countess Helena Cantacuzene, Theodore's cousin, and her young daughter. Both ladies had died captive to the Turks; and Theodore now claimed the county as next of kin. When he approached Salona, accompanied by a detachment of the Knights, the Turks withdrew. Theodore then gave Salona to the Knights in exchange for Corinth. They handed back Kalavryta and abandoned their claims on Mistra when Theodore offered to repay the money that they had given him for the two cities, together with an additional sum to recompense them for the expenses that they had incurred. There was some bickering over the financial details, which caused ill will. But the Knights, who were not given to religious tolerance, had found their Greek subjects so hostile that they abandoned them with some relief. They fared no better with the Greeks of Salona, who refused to co-operate with them against the Turks. Some twelve years later Salona was Turkish once more.

The credit for the diplomatic victory must go to Manuel. Theodore was by now a very sick man. In 1407, when his end was approaching, he took monastic orders, and died a few days later. The inscription over his tomb in the Church of the Brontochion in Mistra calls him 'the brother of our holy Emperor, the monk Theodoret'.

Soon afterwards, the Emperor Manuel composed a funeral oration for his brother. Behind the elegant, careful literary style and the many classical allusions there glows a real affection. He praises Theodore's energy in his younger days; he talks with sympathy of the ill health that clouded Theodore's later years, and he explains the desperate, defeatist transactions with Venice and the Hospital as arising from a real desire to do whatever might be best for Christendom as a whole. Despite this fraternal eulogy Theodore remains a shadowy figure. As a ruler he had been energetic and courageous till illness crippled him and drove him to despair. He was never a very popular prince. But it was not his fault that his reign was filled with wars and raids and devastation. A policy of peace would have been impossible. Like all his family he patronized the arts and played his part in beautifying Mistra. He was not a great scholar, such as Manuel was, but he liked the company of scholars. He seems to have been a devoted husband; and it may be that the Despoena's death was largely responsible for his later melancholy. Whatever his faults, he was loyal and devoted to the Emperor, with whom he was united in a brotherly love that was all too rare in Byzantine history.

VII The Despot Theodore II

THE EMPEROR MANUEL had already made his plans for the succession to the Peloponnesian Despotate. When he knew that his brother was dying he sent his second son, another Theodore, to Mistra to be ready to take over the inheritance; and early in 1408, as soon as he could conveniently leave Constantinople for a while, he came himself to the Peloponnese.

It was a well-timed visit. The Ottoman Sultanate was still in disarray. Its European provinces were in the hands of Bayazet's eldest son, the Emir Suleiman, a man with a liking for the Greeks. In his gratitude for help that Manuel had given to him, he had willingly retroceded Thessalonica and other coastal towns to the Emperor, and in 1404 he accepted as his bride the bastard daughter of the Despot Theodore. So long as he was in power there was no immediate danger to the Christian Empire.

The younger Theodore was now aged about twelve. He, his elder brother John and their next brother Andronicus had been born before Manuel had set out on his Western journey in 1399. Their younger brothers, Constantine, Demetrius and Thomas, were all born after the Emperor's return to Constantinople in 1402. Their mother, Helena, was the daughter of a Serbian prince, Dragas, who had been ruler of Serres and parts of Macedonia till he was defeated and killed by the Turks. Her mother was Greek. Till the Emperor arrived at Mistra it seems that the government was carried on in Theodore II's name by the Protostrator Manuel Phrangopoulos, head of one of the great local families, who had already served as Theodore I's ambassador to Venice. Manuel only stayed long enough in Mistra to assure himself that the child Despot's ministers were administering the government competently and that the restless local nobility obeyed its decrees.

For the next few years the Peloponnese enjoyed a rare tranquillity. So long as the Emir Suleiman ruled over the Turks in Europe they remained at peace with the Greeks. In the peninsula itself the new

Prince of Achaea, Centurione Zaccaria, was too unsure of his position to risk a war with his neighbours. The Venetians were not going to take any action that might interfere with their commerce. In 1410 Suleiman was defeated and slain by his brother Musa, the Emir of Brusa. Musa was of a more aggressive nature and at once demanded back all the territory that Suleiman had ceded to the Greeks. When this was refused he sent an army to attack Thessalonica, while he himself marched on Constantinople. Though he devastated the countryside the walls of both cities defied him, and his fleet was destroyed by the Greeks. Manuel, meanwhile, in the long tradition of Byzantine diplomacy, made contact with Bayazet's youngest son, Mehmet, who was now Emir of Amasea and central Anatolia. Mehmet came to Constantinople, where he saluted the Emperor as his father. His first attempt to oust Musa failed; but in 1413 Musa's troops were routed and he himself captured and strangled. Mehmet became Sultan of the reunited Ottoman dominions. He never forgot his debt to Manuel. So long as he lived the peace endured.

The Peloponnese had been untroubled by Musa's aggression. The young Despot, Theodore II, was now of an age to take over the administration; and Manuel decided to come himself to Mistra to give the boy his parental support. He left Constantinople at the end of July 1414, putting the government in the hands of his son John, whom he had recently crowned co-Emperor. After spending the autumn and winter at Thessalonica, where he had installed his third son, Andronicus, as governor, he arrived at Corinth in March 1415. He was shocked at the state of the fortifications across the Isthmus and at once gave orders that a great wall, with towers at intervals and castles at either end, should be constructed along the line of the Hexamilion. So urgent did he regard the task that it was completed under his supervision in twenty-five days. But it was costly. He hoped that the Venetians would assist with the expense, as the wall would help to protect their Peloponnesian possessions. But the Republic was not prepared to spend money on a project that might, it thought, offend the Turks, with whom it had recently signed a treaty. Besides, only a few years back, in 1407, it had allowed Manuel to take over the considerable sums that his late sister-in-law, the Despoena Bartolomea, had kept on deposit in Venetian banks. It had been generous enough. So, as soon as he arrived in Mistra, Manuel ordered a special levy from the wealthier Peloponnesians. The local nobility, resentful and short-sighted as ever, rose in revolt. Manuel soon crushed the rebel troops in a battle near Kalamata. Order was restored and the tax imposed. The Emperor's prestige was now high. In the autumn of

1415 the Prince of Achaea, Centurione Zaccaria, came to Mistra and paid homage to him as his suzerain.

So long as Sultan Mehmet I was on the Ottoman throne, peace was maintained with the Turks. But Manuel was fearful of the future. He longed to form a solid Christian front against the infidel. The schism between the Orthodox Church and Rome was a constant hindrance to this ideal. Manuel himself was devotedly loyal to his Church; and he knew, too, that his subjects would never willingly submit to Roman domination. It was contrary to their conception of the organization of the Church; and they remembered too vividly the persecution conducted by nearly all the Latin states that emerged after the Fourth Crusade, when their liturgy had been banned and their traditions flouted. The West, on its side, saw no reason for helping people whom it regarded as wilful schismatics. The schism within the papacy itself and the consequent Conciliar movement, which called into question the supreme authority of the Pope, seemed to present the opportunity for some compromise. When the Council of Constance, called to settle the papal problem, met at the end of 1414 there was present an observer, sent by Manuel, the scholar Manuel Chrysoloras, who had been a professor of Greek in Italy and who personally sympathized with the Latin Church. He made an excellent impression and was considered as a possible Pope; but he died while the Council was still in progress. The Pope who was eventually elected in 1418, Martin V, began his reign well disposed towards the Greeks. He offered a special indulgence to Latins who had helped to build and were helping to maintain the Hexamilion wall; and he acceded to a request from Manuel that his sons, all six of them listed by name, should be allowed to marry Catholic brides, stipulating only that the ladies should never be required to change their faith.

In the Peloponnese the religious situation was not acute. In the dwindling Principality of Achaea there were few Latin bishops left. Nearly all the inhabitants, even those of Latin origin, had merged with the local Orthodox. The Venetians kept Latin bishops in their four cities of Corone, Methone, Nauplia and Argos, but they interfered very little with the Orthodox establishment. Only the Archbishop of Patras, who acknowledged no suzerain but the Pope, was aggressively Catholic. But there were still Catholic dynasties in the offing; and there was a close contact with Catholic Italy. Marriage connections with Catholic families might help the Imperial family in its efforts against the Turks. In pursuit of this policy Manuel sought papal help in providing brides for his two oldest sons. The elder, John VIII, had been sent to Mistra in 1416 and had remained there nearly two years, giving support to his brother the Despot and gaining some experience in government. When he returned to Constantinople he found that the wife previously chosen for him by his father, the Russian princess Anna, had died aged fifteen, with the marriage still unconsummated. So Manuel arranged that John should now be provided with a bride from the West, and that one should also be found for Theodore. For John he selected Sophia of Montferrat, the child widow of a Sforza Count of Pavia and herself belonging to the branch of the Palaeologi that had inherited Montferrat. She was well connected, her maternal grandmother having been a daughter of a King of France. For Theodore he seems to have allowed Pope Martin to choose the candidate. She was Cleope Malatesta, the daughter of Malatesta dei Malatesti, lord of Pesaro and Fano, head of a junior branch of the great family that ruled Rimini. She was not of very distinguished birth, but she had two advantages. Her father was on excellent terms with the Venetian government and kept a house in Venice; and she was closely related, probably through her mother, with Pope Martin, who was of the Roman house of Colonna.

The two ladies set sail in a Venetian boat from Chioggia, near Venice, at the end of August 1420. Sophia was married to John, in Constantinople, on 19 January 1421; and the historian Ducas gives us to understand that Cleope's marriage took place there at the same time, though it is possible that she was married at Mistra. Sophia's marriage was a disaster from the outset, owing to her remarkable ugliness. John could not bear the sight of her and kept her hidden away in the back rooms of the palace. After four miserable years she was able to return to Italy, and the marriage was annulled. Soon afterwards, John married a princess of Trebizond, of a family noted for the beauty of its daughters.

Cleope was at first not much more fortunate. The Despot Theodore had grown up to be a strange, neurotic young man, an eager and distinguished scholar who was considered to be one of the best mathematicians of his time. At this period of his life he was not interested in power but wanted to retire to a monastery. He resented the marriage and for two or three years had little to do with his wife. But then there was a reconciliation. Cleope shared her husband's intellectual tastes; and the scholars who gathered at his court all felt a devoted admiration for her, which Theodore came to share. She identified herself completely with her adopted country. Before the marriage Theodore had issued a silver bull in which he guaranteed that Cleope, together with her chaplain and her attendants, should have complete freedom of worship. But in about 1425 Pope Martin received a disquieting letter from one of her ladies-in-waiting, her cousin Battista Malatesta of Montefeltro, complaining that her mistress was being subjected to strong pressure to join the Greek fold, adding that she was suffering many sorrows in her attempt to remain constant in her Catholic faith and that she was being harried by domestic warfare and internal strife. This provoked two stern letters from the Pope, one addressed to Theodore and the other to Cleope. Theodore was strongly urged to support his wife, 'the dearest of all our cousins', in her loyalty to her Church and was advised to copy his late father in his zeal for Church union, a zeal which, in fact, had not been as whole-hearted as the Pope supposed. The letter to Cleope was severe in tone, threatening her with excommunication and damnation should she lapse from the faith. To read it one suspects that the Pope did not quite believe in Battista's protestations of Cleope's fidelity but thought that she had already gone over to the Greeks. In both letters he announced that they were being conveyed by an Augustinian friar, Luca de Offida, who would give the Princess spiritual advice. The Pope's efforts were in vain. When Cleope died her old friend and admirer George Gemistus Plethon composed a moving threnody. 'She followed our rite', he wrote, adding that 'she discarded the soft and decadent habits of the Italians to learn the simple modesty of our own manners, in which she was not excelled by any of our ladies'.

Politically the marriage was equally unproductive. When the Latin archbishop of Patras died in 1424 the Pope appointed to the see his cousin Pandolfo Malatesta, Cleope's brother. But Theodore, who had been on friendly terms with the previous archbishop, was quite indifferent to his brother-in-law, even joining with his brothers in an attack on Patras in 1428. The Venetians were equally disappointed. When in 1429 a dispute arose about the rights of the Venetian citizens in Methone and Corone in the neighbouring countryside, the Republic sent, as its ambassador to Mistra, Cleope's father Malatesta, together with his cousin, the lord of Mantua, whose mother had been a Malatesta. The embassy seems to have achieved nothing. Even the ultimate result of the marriage did nothing to help the papacy. Cleope's only child was a daughter, Helena, born in about 1428, who was given in marriage by her father in 1442 to King John II of Cyprus. She was a violent, neurotic girl, in permanent ill-health; and her main preoccupation till her death in 1458 was to further the cause of the Orthodox Church in Cyprus, at the expense of the Romans.

Under Theodore II and Cleope, Mistra became the leading intellectual centre in the Greek world. But the political situation had darkened again. In 1421 the Emperor Manuel, who was already in his seventies and in failing health, handed over the government of the Empire to his son, John VIII. That same year his friend Sultan Mehmet I died, to be succeeded by his son, Murad I. John VIII, against his father's advice, backed a rival claimant to the Sultanate, quite ineffectually, with the result that Murad in 1422 laid siege to Constantinople and blockaded Thessalonica. Constantinople was saved, it was claimed by the intervention of the city's patroness, the Mother of God, and by the valour of the defence under the young Emperor, though, in fact, it was Manuel's diplomatic intrigues in Anatolia that obliged the Sultan to call off the siege. But Thessalonica was still in danger and was accessible now to the Byzantines only from the sea. Its governor was Manuel's third son, Andronicus, still in his early twenties but already mortally ill with elephantiasis. With the consent of his family and of the city authorities he offered Thessalonica to the Venetians, demanding only that the municipal and religious rights of the citizens be respected. The Republic accepted the offer and took over the city in 1423. The Venetians soon regretted their decision. They neglected the rights of the citizens and the defences of the city. Seven years later, in March 1430, Sultan Murad took Thessalonica by storm.

Soon after the cession of Thessalonica to the Venetians the Emperor John VIII went off to visit Venice and Hungary in a vain attempt to secure aid. He left his aged father in charge of the government in Constantinople. Manuel had recently suffered a stroke, but he was still sufficiently active to conclude a truce with the Sultan, which acknowledged the Turkish conquests but guaranteed the safety of the capital for a few more years. When John VIII returned from his fruitless travels at the end of 1424 Manuel retired into a monastery. He died there in July 1425, aged seventy-five, the most highly respected and most deeply mourned of all the long line of Byzantine emperors.

The Peloponnese had not meanwhile been spared. In 1423 a large Turkish army under Murad's favourite general, Turakhan Bey, advanced to the Isthmus of Corinth. The Despot had vainly been trying to maintain an adequate garrison at the Hexamilion; but the soldiers would not stay there. The Turks passed easily through the defences and marched southward, ravaging as they came. This time the vale of Sparta was not spared. The Turks penetrated to the very walls of Mistra. But it was a raid, not an attempt at conquest. After a few days Turakhan retired, leaving devastation behind him. In 1431 there was another Turkish raid into the peninsula. It seems to have been directed against Arcadia and the Venetian lands in the south-west.

Even without the Turks there was little tranquillity in the Peloponnese in these years. The Despot found himself obliged, in spite of an occasional truce, to fight against Centurione Zaccaria of Achaea and the Navarrese Company. In these petty wars the Greeks kept the upper hand. There was trouble in 1423 and 1424 when Antonio Acciajuoli of Athens tried to occupy Corinth. Further trouble was caused by Theodore I's brother-in-law and rival, Carlo Tocco, lord of Cephallonia and Leucas, who, after having occupied the other Ionian Islands as well as much of Epirus, wished to assert his wife's Peloponnesian claims and bought the port of Clarenza from an Italian adventurer who had captured it. In 1423 John VIII, on his way to Venice, stopped in the Peloponnese and led a successful expedition which forced Tocco to retire behind the walls of Clarenza. Soon afterwards a Greek naval squadron, under the admiral Leontarios, defeated Tocco's fleet in a battle off the Echinades Islands, at the mouth of the Gulf of Patras.

It was therefore natural that the princes of the Imperial dynasty should seek their fortunes in the Peloponnese. Thomas, the youngest of Manuel's sons, had been sent by his father to join Theodore in Mistra in 1418, when he was barely ten years old. He grew up there, at first on friendly terms with Theodore. Andronicus, the third son, came to Mistra on his abandonment of Thessalonica. But he was already a very sick man. He retired almost at once into a monastery and died there four years later. When John VIII was passing through the Peloponnese on his way to Venice in 1423, Theodore, who still resented his marriage and wanted to retire to a monastery, told his brother of his desire. So when John returned to Constantinople he made arrangements for the fourth brother, Constantine, who was ruling the cities of Mesemvria and Anchialos on the Black Sea coast, under the strict suzerainty of the Sultan, to give up that thankless task and take over the government at Mistra. But it was not till 1427 that Constantine reached the Peloponnese; and by that time Theodore was on good terms with Cleope and was enjoying his secular power. He agreed, however, that the province could be subdivided. A successful campaign against Carlo Tocco induced the Cephallonian ruler to come to terms. He offered the hand of his niece, Magdalena, rechristened Theodora, to Constantine, with his city of Clarenza and his Peloponnesian claims as her dowry. To enlarge his appanage Theodore handed over to him the Greek possessions in Messenia and the Mani, as well as Vostitsa (Aigion) on the northern shore of the peninsula. The division of territory was supervised by John VIII, who made a special visit from Constantinople to see that Constantine, his favourite brother, received a worthy appanage. At the same time

Thomas, the youngest brother, was given a small appanage based on Kalavryta.

No sooner had Constantine married Theodora Tocco than the brothers joined together to march against Patras, whose lord, Archbishop Pandolfo Malatesta, Theodore's brother-in-law, was away in Italy seeking help for his precarious see. The attack was not pressed hard; and the princes retired after extracting tribute from the citizens. Soon afterwards, John VIII returned to Constantinople; and Constantine determined to secure Patras for himself.

Of the six sons of Manuel, Constantine was by far the most vigorous and energetic. He had a personal charm that enslaved his friend, the historian George Sphrantzes; and he was to prove his nobility and courage by his death before the walls of Constantinople. But his political sense was not always wise. When he proposed to attack Patras again the next year he risked the enmity not only of Venice, which was alarmed by the Greek revival and had no wish to see the Despots controlling any of the major seaports of the Peloponnese, but also of the Sultan, who chose to regard Patras, and, indeed, all Greece as being under his suzerainty. Theodore disapproved of the venture, not because of jealousy of his brother, as Sphrantzes supposed, though there may have been a touch of it, and certainly not from any love of his brother-in-law, the Archbishop; but his policy was to keep on good terms both with Venice and the Sultan as far as it was practicable. His fears were unfounded, for the time being. When Constantine entered Patras in June 1429, there was no reaction from Venice; and an embassy headed by Sphrantzes hurried to the Sultan's court to obtain his consent to the conquest. It was granted; but the Turks marked Constantine as a likely source of danger for the future. The Archbishop's troops held out in the castle for a few more months; and he himself hired a company of Catalan adventurers to aid him. They surprised and captured Constantine's capital of Clarenza and only departed when they were given the sum of six thousand ducats, none of which they handed over to their employer.

While Constantine advanced on Patras his brother Thomas attacked the ailing Prince of Achaea, Centurione Zaccaria, and his dwindling company of Navarrese. When Venice refused him help Centurione gave up the struggle. He had only one legitimate child, a daughter, Catherine. He offered her in marriage to Thomas, with all his possessions as her dowry, except for the lordship of Arkadia, the town of Kyparissia and its district, which he reserved for himself and his wife. The treaty was signed in September 1429. The next spring Thomas and Catherine were married at Mistra. Centurione died in

1432. Thomas at once marched on Kyparissia and thrust his mother-in-law into prison, where she remained for the rest of her days.

The whole of the Peloponnese was now at last in Greek hands, except for the four Venetian towns, Corone, Methone, Nauplia and Argos. It was divided between the three brothers, whose territories were readjusted in 1432, to suit the circumstances. Thomas, who had been given the title of Despot in 1430, exchanged his capital of Kalavryta for Constantine's capital of Clarenza and took over Constantine's lands in the south-west, which marched with his inheritance from Centurione. Constantine, who had recently taken over Corinth from Theodore, received the whole north of the peninsula, which suited him, as he had ambitions to extend his lands on the further side of the Isthmus of Corinth. Theodore retained the south-east, the vale of Sparta and most of the centre. He had no authority over his brothers, only a precedence of honour. But Mistra remained the supreme capital, the home of the dynasty. It was to Mistra that the corpse of Constantine's young wife, Theodora Tocco, was brought for burial after her death in November 1429. It was at Mistra that the marriage of Thomas and Catherine Zaccaria was celebrated. It was at Mistra that the scholars of the Greek world gathered, to bask in the patronage of Theodore and Cleope.

Apart from the Turkish invasion of 1431, the Peloponnese entered a period of peace. The three Despots might disagree over policy, and there was little co-operation between them; but there was no active breach. Cleope seems to have provided a harmonious influence. Her death in 1433, while she was probably still in her twenties, was mourned by all the Greek scholars of the time and deeply sorrowed her husband, who had come to value and love her. His neurosis increased and his relations with his brothers deteriorated. To some extent this was inevitable. By 1435 the question of the succession to the Empire had arisen. John VIII had been married for six years to his princess from Trebizond; but, happy though the marriage was, it was childless. Theodore, as the next brother in age to John, considered that his was the best claim. John wished for Constantine as his successor; and Constantine was eager to have the throne. In the autumn of 1435 Constantine went to Constantinople to secure official recognition as the Emperor's heir. While there he sent his faithful secretary, Sphrantzes, to the Turkish court, in a vain attempt to engage the Sultan's support. The next spring Theodore came to Constantinople to discover what was happening. There were angry scenes between the brothers. Theodore was ready to fight for his rights; and both brothers returned to the Peloponnese prepared for war. Skirmishes had already broken out between their troops when a peace mission arrived from Constantinople, proposing a temporary compromise. John VIII was about to go to Italy, to attend a Council for the union of the Churches of Constantinople and Rome. It was decided that Constantine should act as his regent in Constantinople in his absence, and in the meantime Theodore would administer Constantine's lands in the Peloponnese.

The holding of the Union Council, which met first at Ferrara and was then moved to Florence, added to the disagreement between the brothers. John had decided that the West would never give effective help to Byzantium unless Byzantium accepted the authority of the Church of Rome. He was interested in theology; but theology had now to serve a political purpose. He went to Italy determined that this should be achieved. Constantine, who was the least intellectual of the brothers, agreed with the Emperor on the necessity of union. Thomas seems to have early acquired Roman sympathies, perhaps from his wife, to whom he was devoted. Theodore followed the example of his father Manuel, behaving with friendly courtesy towards the Roman Church but avoiding any proposal for union. His private life showed where his sympathies lay. Not only did his wife join his Church, but he brought up his daughter, the future Queen of Cyprus, to be staunchly Orthodox. The fifth brother, Demetrius, who had been living in Constantinople, was a passionate opponent of union. It was probably to keep an eye on him that John insisted on his joining the party bound for Italy.

Constantine left for Constantinople to take up the regency in September 1437; and John and Demetrius left two months later for Italy. John returned to Constantinople early in 1440; but it was not till the summer of 1441 that Constantine left Constantinople for the Peloponnese, pausing on the way to marry Catherine Gattilusi, a princess of the Hellenized Genoese dynasty that had ruled for more than a century over the island of Lesbos. During the intervening years the Peloponnese enjoyed another of its rare intervals of tranquillity. There seem to have been no foreign invasions or raids; and, with Constantine absent, Theodore and Thomas were ready to live in peace with each other. Constantine's return strained but did not upset the peace. He was summoned back to Constantinople in the summer of 1442 when the Emperor believed that their anti-unionist brother, Demetrius, who had been given a small appanage at Selymbria, on the Sea of Marmora, to keep him out of the capital, was plotting to attack the city with the help of the Sultan, who equally disapproved of the union, for purely political reasons. On his way, Constantine visited Lesbos to help drive off a Turkish naval attack. There his wife, who had come with him to see her family, died quite suddenly, leaving him once more a childless widower.

John VIII was only in his early fifties, but he was a sick and weary man. He had come back from Italy to find his lovely Empress dead of the plague; and the union of the Churches, to which he had committed himself and his people, was greeted with such sullen enmity that he could not enforce it. He needed his vigorous brother's help. At Constantine's request he gave him Demetrius's appanage of Selymbria. From there Constantine was well placed to aid his brother while he lived and to take over the throne when he died. But he too seems to have become depressed and disillusioned by life in Constantinople and to have yearned for the greater scope provided by the Greek peninsula. When in the summer of 1443 envoys from Theodore arrived at the Imperial court to propose that Constantine should exchange Selymbria with him for Mistra, Constantine and the Emperor both agreed. It is likely that the settlement was advised by the Dowager Empress Helena, a lady whom her sons deeply respected and who may well have thought that Theodore would handle the religious problem with greater tact than Constantine. Before the end of the year Constantine was installed at Mistra and Theodore had left the Peloponnese for his little appanage at Selymbria.

Theodore II had reigned at Mistra for thirty-six years. They had been difficult years. In his earlier days he had had to deal with unruly nobles and constant frontier wars; and the Turks were always lurking in the background. But the nobility had been tamed and, thanks more to his brothers than himself, the peninsula had been cleared of the Latins. But his own diplomacy had helped in dealing with Venice and with the Turks. When he left his lands, agriculture and commerce both were flourishing. He has been unfairly treated by history, chiefly because he was disparaged by the great historian of his family, George Sphrantzes. Sphrantzes's devotion to Theodore's brother Constantine was well justified by his hero's vigour and courage, but it led him to dislike and to underrate anyone with whom Constantine disagreed. Owing to the brilliance of his writing his verdicts have been accepted. Theodore was not an easy man, with his moodiness and his streak of religiosity. His wife had a hard time at first; but the marriage was happy in the end. Theodore held the admiration and affection of the leading Greek scholars of his time. It was under his patronage at Mistra that philosophy and letters flourished for the last time in Byzantium.

Theodore was never allowed the supreme chance of proving his ability. For nearly five years he waited at Selymbria for the day when he would ascend the Imperial throne. But in 1448 his health began to fail, and he died in June, four months before the brother whom he had hoped to succeed. The succession was left after all to Constantine.

VIII   The Last Despots

UNDER the Despot Constantine the Greeks of the Peloponnese had their last taste of glory. On his arrival at Mistra at the end of 1443 he at once set about the reorganization of his dominion. He seems to have adjusted his frontier with his brother Thomas, with whom he was on good terms, giving him much of the centre of the peninsula. In consequence Thomas moved his court to Leontarion, in the south of Arcadia, where he could keep in close touch with Mistra. From his circle of able and devoted friends Constantine chose governors for the more important cities. At the same time he restored to the local nobility many of the powers and privileges which his predecessors had taken from them. This was a dangerous policy; but for the moment it enabled him, it seems, to induce them to help in paying for his first major task, the rebuilding of the Hexamilion wall, which the Turks had destroyed in 1423.

With the defences of the peninsula repaired, Constantine, to whom a life of military glory was preferable to one of peaceful administration, prepared to cross into continental Greece. The moment was well chosen. He was in touch with Rome and knew that Pope Eugenius IV was planning a Crusade, to reward the Byzantines for having subscribed to the Union of Florence. He knew too that Sultan Murad was planning to abdicate his throne and retire into a life of contemplation. In the spring of 1444 a great Crusading army set out, led by King Vladislav of Hungary and his commander-in-chief, John Hunyadi, and joined by George Branković, Prince of Serbia, a vassal of the Sultan's, and by the Albanian chieftain, George Castriota, known as Scanderbeg. While they advanced far into the Balkans, distracting the Turks, Constantine marched across the Isthmus into Attica, capturing Athens and Thebes and forcing Nerio II Acciajuoli, Duke of Athens, to do him homage. Nerio's appeals to the Sultan, who was his suzerain, were unheeded. But the King of Hungary's Crusade halted. The troops that the papal legate, Cardinal Cesarini, brought to join it were fewer than he had expected; and the Sultan was gathering a great army to meet him. But neither Sultan nor King wanted a pitched battle. In June 1444, they signed a ten years' truce, each solemnly swearing to maintain it, and not to cross the Danube. The Sultan returned home to prepare for his retirement. The Cardinal, who had been furious at the truce, persuaded the King that an oath sworn to an infidel was invalid. When news came that Murad had crossed to Asia the Crusader army advanced again, but reduced in size; for George Branković and Scanderbeg refused to condone the perjury, and at Constantinople the Emperor John proclaimed his horror at it. Sultan Murad, righteously incensed, returned to Europe with an army far larger than the Christian. The Crusaders reached Varna on the Black Sea in November. There the Turks fell on them and routed them. The King and the Cardinal were killed. Only Hunyadi and a handful of Hungarians escaped. Soon the Turks were back on the Danube.

The events of the summer had encouraged Constantine; and the Turks' victory at Varna had come too late in the year for them to take action in Greece before the spring. When the spring arrived Sultan Murad had retired into a mystic's cell, and his twelve-year-old successor, a precocious and opinionated boy, had quarrelled with his father's ministers and had earned the loathing of his army. In the Balkans Scanderbeg was driving back the Turks, with help from Hunyadi. Constantine felt secure enough to continue his campaign. In the spring of 1445, with the additional help of a few but well armed troops sent to him on the Pope's suggestion by the Duke of Burgundy, he again crossed the Isthmus and, after confirming his hold over Athens and Thebes, marched up through Phocis into the Pindus range, displacing various small Turkish garrisons as he passed by and ravaging the countryside, to the detriment of its Greek inhabitants. The Vlach tribes of the southern Pindus came to pay him homage and to receive a Vlach governor from him. He then came down to the Gulf of Corinth and marched back along its northern shore, driving the Venetian governor out of the prosperous port of Vitrinitsa. When he returned in triumph across the Isthmus his general, John Cantacuzenus, carried on the campaign in Phocis.

The triumph was short-lived. In the late summer of 1446 Murad was persuaded by his former ministers to come out of his retirement and deal with the enemies of the Sultanate. He made it his first task to punish Constantine. In November, despite the lateness of the season, he himself appeared in Greece at the head of a great army. All Constantine's recent conquests fell into his hands; and the Duke of Athens received him as a deliverer. Constantine was isolated. After his attack on Venetian possessions he could not expect any help from Venice; and there was no one else in a position to help him. As the Turks approached the Hexamilion he sent the young historian Laonicus Chalcocondyles as ambassador to Murad, to ask for peace terms. Murad demanded the destruction of the Hexamilion, and when that was refused cast the ambassador into prison. Constantine, with his brother Thomas at his side, determined to hold the walls. They were strong and well garrisoned. Constantine had brought up all his available forces, perhaps some twenty thousand men; but many of them were Albanians who were notoriously unreliable. The Turks had cannon with them; and, though the wall stood up well to the bombardment, the defenders were obliged to keep under cover. The siege lasted for a fortnight. At last, on 10 December, the Turks were able to swarm up on to the ramparts, and the defence collapsed. The Despots' army disintegrated. They themselves barely escaped with their lives.

After destroying the Hexamilion, Murad led the main Turkish army through Corinth, past Sikyon and Vostitsa (Aigion) to Patras, burning the towns and villages as he passed. He found Patras deserted. The population had fled across the gulf to Naupaktos; but he did not trouble to attack it and marched on to Clarenza. Meanwhile, a second army under Turakhan Bey marched towards Mistra; but, no doubt owing to the difficulty of crossing the mountains in the wintry weather, it seems that he did not reach the vale of Sparta. He eventually turned west to join the Sultan at Clarenza. During the last days of the year the great Turkish army moved slowly northward, leaving ruins in its wake and dragging with it a multitude of captives, estimated by Greek and by Italian sources independently at sixty thousand, all destined for the slave-markets of the East.

The disastrous outcome of his policy cooled the ardour of the Despot Constantine. He spent the year 1447 quietly seeking to repair some of the damage. It was in one way fortunate that the invasion had taken place in winter. Buildings had been destroyed and the inhabitants left homeless; but the crops had not been harmed. The traveller Cyriacus of Ancona, who passed through the Peloponnese in the summer of 1447, was impressed by the richness of the harvest. Meanwhile, Constantine and Thomas made their humble submission to the Sultan. They were ordered to pay him a large annual tribute; and the Hexamilion was not to be repaired.

In the spring of 1448 news reached Mistra of the death of the Despot Theodore. Constantine could now confidently expect to inherit the Imperial crown; and, with his ambitions in Greece brought to nothing, he was ready for the burden. The Emperor John VIII died on 31 October 1448. On his deathbed he had ordered that Constantine should succeed him. But Constantine was far away. Close at hand there was the Despot Demetrius, who had inherited the Selymbrian appanage on Theodore's death and who was liked by the populace of Constantinople because of his steadfast opposition to Church union. He arrived in the city to stake his claim. The situation was resolved by the aged Empress-Mother, using her constitutional authority as a crowned Empress in default of a crowned Emperor. Constantine was her eldest surviving son. He was abler than his brothers and, though she did not wholly like his religious policy, he was probably her favourite; he bore as his second name her family surname of Dragases. His secretary Sphrantzes happened to be in Constantinople, visiting his son who was lying sick there. The Empress sent him at once to the Sultan's court to obtain Murad's approval of Constantine's succession. The Despot Thomas was already on his way to Constantinople at the time of John's death. When he arrived there on 13 November and gave his support to the Empress, Demetrius saw that he was beaten. Both brothers joined with their mother in proclaiming Constantine as Emperor.

It was necessary that he should be crowned as soon as possible. Breaking with all precedent the Empress ordered two high officials, Alexius Lascaris Philanthropenus and Manuel Palaeologus Iagrus, to go to Mistra, bearing with them the Imperial crown. There, on 6 January 1449, the Metropolitan of Lacedemonia placed the crown on Constantine's head. It must have been a strange ceremony. We do not know whether it took place in the Metropolitan Church of St Demetrius, a small building for containing the congregation that must have been present, or in the even smaller building of St Sophia, the Palace Church. No doubt the notables of the Peloponnese, the Despot's garrison and the citizens of the small city played the role of the Senate, the army and the people of Constantinople in making the ceremonial acclamations. It was the greatest occasion in the history of Mistra, but a sad occasion; for the new Emperor was leaving his people in the Peloponnese to take command of an Empire that was doomed.

Though everyone accepted Constantine as Emperor, some purists doubted whether the coronation was really valid. But a coronation in Constantinople, where the unionist Patriarch was cold-shouldered by most of his clergy and the public refused to enter St Sophia if he officiated there, would have been disastrous. The Metropolitan of Lacedemonia bore no such stigma.

A few weeks after the coronation Constantine left Mistra for ever. He sailed to Constantinople in a Catalan ship and arrived there on 12 March. One of his first duties was to arrange for the future of the Peloponnese. After a number of family discussions and arguments it was decided that Demetrius and Thomas should share the province between them, the dividing line being drawn fairly straight from the north-east to the south-west of the peninsula. Thomas received the north-western half, including the cities of Sikyon, Patras, Kalavryta and Clarenza, and the Achaean plain, as well as Messenia and Kalamata. Demetrius received Mistra; and his possessions were to include Corinth in the north, Karytaina in the centre and the Mani in the south. The two brothers attended a ceremony in the presence of the Emperor and the Empress-Mother, at which they swore allegiance to the Emperor and swore, too, that they would remain at peace with each other. When this was done Thomas returned to his dominions in August and Demetrius followed him to the Peloponnese some three weeks later. The settlement was endorsed by the Sultan, who sent all three brothers assurances of his benevolence.

It was too much to expect Demetrius and Thomas to live for long in amity. They hardly knew each other, as Thomas had lived almost entirely in the Peloponnese since his early childhood; and they held opposing views on the crucial question of religion. From the outset they refused to co-operate. When the Venetians sent to complain to the Despots of the incursions that their Albanian soldiers continually made into the lands surrounding the Venetian cities, each Despot sent a separate embassy to the Republic. Demetrius's envoys received better treatment in Venice than did those of Thomas; but the Venetians refused to give Demetrius any support in his quarrels with his brother.

Demetrius needed support; for Thomas soon broke the family compact and occupied the plain of Scorta, in the centre of Arcadia. To obtain redress Demetrius had to apply to the Sultan, who sent Turakhan Bey to look into the matter. As Thomas refused to give up Scorta, Turakhan ordered him to hand over Kalamata and Messenia in compensation to his brother. War between the Despots was thus avoided; but they remained on cool terms with each other.

Sultan Murad died in February 1451. His son, Mehmet II, on his accession sent to assure the Emperor and the Despots of his goodwill. Unfortunately Constantine believed the new Sultan to be the same arrogant and unwise boy who had temporarily occupied the throne six years previously. Mehmet had grown up. He was now an ambitious and able young man, clear in his aims but devious and secret in his methods. Only those who knew him well understood that he was determined above all to conquer Constantinople. Constantine, believing Mehmet to have difficulties in Anatolia, sent him a somewhat haughty complaint about the incursions of Turkish soldiers into Byzantine territory. Mehmet retorted by breaking off relations with the Emperor and openly set about his preparations for the siege of the great city.

No help was to come to Constantinople from the Peloponnese. In October 1452, the Sultan ordered Turakhan Bey, now a very old man, with his sons Omar and Ahmet, to invade the peninsula . The Turks broke easily through the defences of the Hexamilion. Throughout the winter months they ravaged the villages of the countryside but made no attempt to capture the larger towns, except for Neocastron, which fell into their hands, and Siderokastro, which successfully resisted them. The Greeks still possessed one good general, Matthew Asen, whose sister Theodora was wife of the Despot Demetrius. Matthew lured part of the Turkish army, under the command of Ahmet Bey, into a narrow defile, where he fell upon it and routed it, taking Ahmet prisoner. After this set-back the Turks retired. But it was too late to send any succour to Constantinople, even if succour could have deen spared.

The fall of Constantinople, in May 1453, brought mourning to the whole Greek world; and the citizens of Mistra remembered with sorrow but with pride the noble Emperor who had lived so long amongst them and who now had perished at the gates of his Imperial city. The outcome for the Peloponnese was further trouble. For more than a century past, numbers of Albanians had come into the peninsula. The Despots Manuel Cantacuzenus and Theodore I had welcomed them. Not only were they hard-working farmers who were ready to take over desolate land but, still more usefully, they were fine fighting-men who soon formed the greater part of the Despots' armies. But they kept themselves separate from the local population, whom they despised. Now, at this low tide in Greek fortunes, with neither Demetrius nor Thomas commanding the loyalty that they had felt for earlier Despots, they rose in revolt. They had no native leader whom they all trusted. So the rebels in Thomas's dominion took as their chief John Asan Centurione, bastard son of the last Latin Prince of Achaea. He had attempted a revolt some years previously and had been captured and imprisoned by Thomas, but had recently escaped with the help of a clever Greek, Nicephorus Loukanis, who remained his chief adviser. In Demetrius's lands the rebels chose as leader Manuel Cantacuzenus, a grandson of the Despot Matthew, whose family had always resented the supersession of their family by the Palaeologi. Manuel had been local governor of Maina and had many friends among the local Greek nobility, who now joined in the revolt. Soon one rebel army was besieging Thomas at Patras, while the other was encamped before the walls of Mistra. In despair the two Despots sent for help from their overlord the Sultan. Sultan Mehmet had no wish to see a bellicose Albanian state established in the Peloponnese and providing an opportunity for intervention from the West. Once again Turakhan Bey was told to enter the peninsula. His son, Omar Bey, whom he sent with an army in December 1453, managed to check the rebels but not to suppress them. It was not till Turakhan arrived himself the next summer that the revolt was finally crushed. The bastard Zaccaria prince fled to Venetian territory and ended his life in Italy. Manuel Cantacuzenus, whom the Albanians called Ghin, found his way to Ragusa and died in Hungary. Loukanis saved himself by taking service under Demetrius's brother-in-law, Matthew Asen.

The Despots were restored, and were ordered to show their humble gratitude by paying the Sultan an annual tribute of ten or twelve thousand ducats each. But meanwhile, the leading Greek families of the peninsula sent to Mehmet to ask to be placed directly under his administration. He graciously consented; and as a result the Despots could not raise any taxes from their wealthier subjects. In spite of the wars and raids there were parts of the country that were still prosperous. The silk industry was still maintained in Achaea and had more recently been successfully established in the vale of Sparta. But the revenues that it brought in were insufficient to pay for the Despots' households and government. There was none to spare for the tribute. Matters were not improved by the mutual quarrels of the Despots. Thomas still hopefully believed that Western powers could be persuaded to intervene to rescue the Peloponnese. To Demetrius, who was more practical, the only chance of preserving any autonomy was by subservience to the all-powerful Turk.

By 1458 the tribute due to the Sultan was three years in arrears. He was not pleased. He was also irritated by Thomas's intrigues with the West. He had been alarmed when he learnt that at the time of the Albanian revolt Venice had contemplated aid to the rebels. It would not suit him to have any Western power interfering in the Peloponnese, especially if he would need it as his base were he ever to achieve his ambition of invading Italy. The Despots, especially Thomas, must be taught a lesson. In May 1458, Mehmet himself led a great army across the ruined Hexamilion and advanced on Corinth. Corinth formed part of Demetrius's principality; and he had recently appointed his brother-in-law, Matthew Asen, as its governor. When the invasion started Matthew was away visiting the Despot; but, despite his absence, the garrison of Acrocorinth, the great rock-fortress in which the citizens now crowded (for the ravages of war had left the lower city uninhabitable), decided to resist and drove off the first attacks. A few days later Matthew Asen, with seventy companions, succeeded in creeping through the Turkish lines by night and climbing up the citadel rock, bringing with him useful supplies of arms and corn. The resistance of Acrocorinth probably saved Demetrius's other lands from attack. Mehmet was obliged to leave a large part of his army to blockade the citadel. With the rest of his army he set off to ravage Thomas's territory, turning down into Arcadia, and towards Messenia. Thomas fled with his family to the little port of Mantinea, south of Kalamata, ready to sail to Italy. Demetrius had retired to Monemvasia. Mehmet, who had heard of the impregnability of Monemvasia, longed to go and test its strength, but decided more prudently not to enter Laconia. He went northward to attack the fortress-town of Mouchli, near Tegea, of which Demetrius Asen, another brother-in-law of the Despot Demetrius, was governor. It was fiercely defended but had to capitulate when the Sultan cut off its water-supply. After leaving a small garrison there Mehmet moved swiftly to the north coast, capturing Kalavryta, then Vostitsa and Patras, in all of which he placed a garrison. He then returned to Corinth. Matthew Asen was still holding out in Acrocorinth; but supplies were now very short. At the end of August the Metropolitan, who could not bear to see his flock starving, persuaded Matthew that he must yield. The Sultan allowed the garrison to leave the fortress with full military honours. Matthew himself was sent to give the Despots his peace terms. Demetrius was to cede Corinth and Thomas about a third of his territory, including Patras, Vostitsa and Kalavryta. They were to pay an annual tribute of 3,000 pieces of gold. The Despots had no choice but to submit to these terms. In October the Sultan and his army withdrew, bringing with them many thousands of prisoners, men, women and children. Most of them were sent to settle in Constantinople, which the Sultan was anxious to re-populate. Turakhan's son, Omar Bey, was left as Turkish governor of the Peloponnese, residing at Corinth.

Demetrius, thankful that Mistra, at least, had been spared, was ready to abide by the peace. Thomas still hoped for Western aid. On 1 June 1459, Pope Pius II opened a Council at Mantua, at which the Greek-born Cardinal Bessarion made an impassioned plea for help to the Peloponnese against the infidel. His pleading was received with enthusiasm but without any practical consequences. He then went with other papal envoys to preach the Crusade in Germany, equally unsuccessfully. However, in June the Pope himself managed to hire and equip two hundred soldiers and the Duchess of Milan, Bianca Maria Sforza, added another hundred to them. When they arrived, Thomas set out at once with them and his own troops to attack Patras. The attack was unsuccessful, though he managed to recapture Kalavryta. But then the Italians began to wander home; and Thomas thought that it would be more profitable to invade his brother's territory. Demetrius was taken by surprise. His own subjects did nothing to defend themselves. The Sultan, who was busy on his northern frontier, ordered a small detachment to join Omar's garrisons. But it was weakened by disease; and it was some time before Omar could restore order and Matthew Asen repulse Thomas. On the Turks' orders and through the mediation of the Metropolitan of Lacedemonia, the Despots met at Kastritsa in the autumn and swore to live in peace with each other. But the peace was brief. Thomas seems to have refused to restore to Demetrius some of his towns, and Demetrius therefore attacked him. Desultory fighting continued through the winter months.

By the spring of 1460 the Sultan had had enough. He assembled an army, and in mid-May he arrived with it at Corinth. The Despot Demetrius was summoned to meet him there. He was afraid to make the journey. Some eighteen months previously he had been told to send his daughter Helena to enter the Sultan's harem. She was his only child; and he did not wish her to suffer such a fate. He had been hoping to marry her to an Aragonese prince, the heir of the Duke of Calabria, but the negotiations had been held up owing to the death in 1458 of the intended bridegroom's uncle, King Alfonso of Naples. He could not disobey the Sultan's command. So he prevaricated, meanwhile sending her with her mother to the safety of Monemvasia. Instead of going himself to meet the Sultan he despatched Matthew Asen, whom he knew that the Sultan respected, with sumptuous gifts. Mehmet was not pleased. Matthew was put under arrest; and a Turkish army was sent to march straight on Mistra.

On 29 May 1460, seven years to the day after the fall of Constantinople, the citizens of Mistra could look across the valley and watch the great Turkish army wind its way down the slopes of Parnon. Next morning it was encamped outside the city walls. There was no opposition. With the army the Sultan had sent his Greek secretary, Thomas Katavolenos. He persuaded the Despot to yield without resistance and to abandon his plan to escape himself to Monemvasia.

On 31 May the Sultan himself arrived before Mistra; and the Despot was invited to his tent. He was honourably received. As he entered the tent Mehmet rose from his seat and led Demetrius to a chair by his side. Demetrius was terrified; but the Sultan spoke to him gently and kindly, promising him an appanage in Thrace, to compensate him for his lost principality. However, he was told to summon his wife and daughter from Monemvasia. When they arrived at Mistra the two ladies were put into the care of eunuchs in the Sultan's entourage, while the Despot was obliged to accompany the Sultan when after four days at Mistra he set out to conquer the rest of the peninsula.

The conquest was quickly achieved. While the Sultan paid a ceremonial visit to the Venetian cities of Methone and Corone, his main army, under Zaganos Pasha, a renegade Greek, swept through Laconia and Arcadia. In Demetrius's dominions two fortified towns, Karditsa and Gardiki, attempted to resist. Their capture was followed by massacres of the men and the captivity of the women and children. The Sultan was not disposed to be clement. But Zaganos overdid the cruelty, often in breach of Muslim law, which forbade the slaughter or imprisonment of those who made a voluntary submission. In many towns the citizens preferred to die fighting rather than face his savagery. The Sultan soon replaced him by Mehmet Pasha, a renegade of Peloponnesian stock, who showed some sympathy for the vanquished. One town alone successfully defied the Turks, Salmenikon, between Vostitsa and Patras. Its governor, Constantine Palaeologus Graitzas, held out in the citadel till July 1461, when he surrendered with full military honours. Mehmet Pasha declared later that Graitzas was the only 'man' whom he encountered in the Peloponnese.

The Despot Thomas and his Western friends had done nothing to help Salmenikon. While Demetrius followed miserably in the Sultan's train, Thomas and his family cowered in the little Messenian town of Porto Longo, close to Methone, having prudently brought with them the relics of St Andrew from Patras. In July 1460, they set sail for Corfu. The Princess and her children remained there, while Thomas went with his precious relics to Italy, to present them to the Pope, whose pensioner he became. He died in 1465. His younger son, Manuel, fled soon afterwards from Rome, where the Pope had reduced his pension, to Constantinople, where the Sultan was more generous to him. Of his two sons, one died young and the other became a Muslim, ending his days as Mehmet Pasha. Neither left children. Thomas's elder son, whose pension was larger, remained in Rome, calling himself 'Imperator Constantinopolitanus'. But he offended his patrons by marrying a lady from the streets. He died in

1502, having sold his Imperial claims first to Charles VIII of France and subsequently to Ferdinand and Isabella of Spain. He was said to have left a son called Constantine, who for a time commanded the Papal Guard but died in obscurity. Of Thomas's daughters the elder, Helena, was already the widow of a Serbian prince, Lazar III Branković. She had three daughters. One was married as a child to the King of Bosnia, and disappeared into a Turkish harem when her adopted country was conquered by the Sultan. One married the lord of Cephallonia but died a few months later. The third married the son of the Albanian chieftain, Scanderbeg. Thomas's younger daughter, Zoe, was brought up at the papal court after her father's death and was married at the age of ten to a Prince Caracciolo, who died soon afterwards. In 1472, when she was sixteen, the Pope arranged for her marriage to the Tsar of Muscovy, Ivan III, hoping thereby to convert Russia to Catholicism. But Zoe, re-christened Sophia, became an ardent champion of Orthodoxy. She led a full and stormy life in Russia, dying in 1503. She had six sons and a daughter who became Queen of Poland. Tsar Ivan the Terrible was her grandson.

The Despot Demetrius was given by the Sultan an appanage which consisted of the islands of Imbros and Lemnos, with parts of Thasos and Samothrace, and the Thracian town of Enos. He lived at Enos for seven years, with his wife and her brother, Matthew Asen, enjoying a large income, most of which he gave to the Church. Then suddenly they were disgraced. Sphrantzes, who hated Matthew and was never fair to him in his memoirs, declared that Matthew, who was in charge of the local salt monopoly, had allowed his underlings to cheat the Sultan's government over revenue. Mehmet was furious when this was discovered and stripped Demetrius of his appanage and his revenues. The family went to live in penury at Didymoticon, where Matthew seems to have died. Then the Sultan took pity on Demetrius and installed him and his wife with a small but adequate income in a house in Adrianople. His daughter Helena was living there. The Sultan had never taken her into his harem. He feared, it was said, that being a high-spirited girl she might try to poison him. She was given her own establishment and a large allowance, but was forbidden to marry. She died probably in 1469, still in her twenties, leaving all her possessions to the Patriarch of Constantinople. Her parents were so grief-stricken at her death that each of them retired into monastic life. They both died in 1470, Demetrius a few months before his wife.

The only princess to have been born at Mistra, Helena, daughter of Theodore II, and wife of the King of Cyprus, had already died in 1458, before her native city had fallen to the infidel.

By the late summer of 1461 the whole Peloponnese was in Turkish hands, except for the Venetian colonies of Methone and Corone, Argos and Nauplia, for the wilder parts of the Mani peninsula, into which the conquerors did not dare to penetrate, and for the town of Monemvasia. On Demetrius's surrender to the Sultan, the Monemvasiots, under their governor Manuel Palaeologus, considered themselves to be Thomas's subjects. But he soon fled from the country and even contemplated offering the fortress to the Sultan in return for some city on the west coast of Greece. The citizens then accepted a passing Catalan pirate, Lope de Baldaja, as their lord; but he proved to be both tyrannical and incompetent and was soon ejected. Next, apparently on Thomas's suggestion, they put themselves under the protection of his patron, Pope Pius II, stipulating only that their Orthodoxy should be respected. But the Pope, after installing a Catholic archbishop, took little further interest in the city. So in 1464 the citizens accepted the sovereignty of the Venetian Republic.

Venice, however, was unable to preserve her Peloponnesian possessions for long. Argos had already fallen to the Turks in 1462, and Methone and Corone fell to them in 1500. In 1540, after a disastrous war, Venice ceded to the Sultan the uncaptured fortresses of Nauplia and Monemvasia.

The Greeks of the Peloponnese still rebelled now and then against their Turkish masters, vainly hoping for help from Venice or some other Western power. Each rebellion ended in disaster. For the most part the Peloponnesians reconciled themselves to infidel dominion. At Mistra itself everything was calm and orderly, with a Turkish governor in residence in the Palace of the Despots.

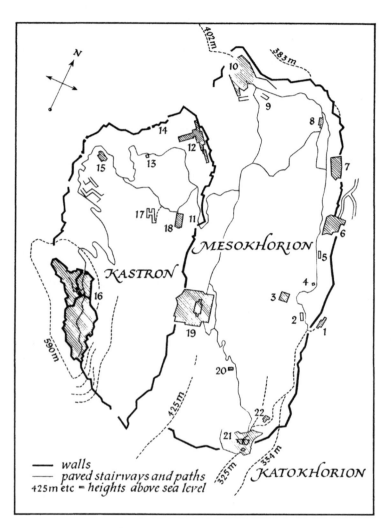

Mistra **1** Marmara, **2** Church of St Christopher, **3** Lascaris mansion, **4** well, **5** passage, **6** fortification, **7** Metropolitan Church, **8** Church of the Evanghelistria, **9** Church of the Sts Theodore, **10** Hodeghetria Church, **11** Monemvasia Gate, **12** Palace of the Despots, **13** chapel, **14** Nauplia Gate, **15** Church of St Sophia, **16** castle, **17** Palataki, **18** Church of St Nicholas, **19** Pantanassa, **20** Phrangopoulos mansion, **21** Church of the Peribleptos, **22** Church of St George

IX The City of Mistra

It is not easy nowadays to envisage Mistra as it must have been under the Despots. Today its charm to the visitor lies in its quiet and the beauty of its setting. One leaves the bustle of modern life in the pleasant little town that lies a mile to the south. In the old walled city climbing up the steep mountainside only a few churches stand out intact as buildings, and the great shell of the Palace of the Despots still dominates the middle scene. The only residents are the nuns who occupy the convent of the Pantanassa, apart from the officials who man by day the little museum and offices down by the Metropolitan Church. It is hard to remember that this was once a lively city of some twenty thousand inhabitants and with populous suburbs below the hill. But as one wanders through the ruined streets and alleyways one begins to see what must have been the great houses of the nobility, the poorer houses, the shops and the barracks, though much remains unidentified.

The old city was in three sections. From the castle on the summit of the hill, walls stretched down the slope on either side to just below the Palace of the Despots, where they were united by a third wall, thus forming a very rough triangle. Below this triangle there was a slightly larger section going down to the bottom of the hill and shaped like a sort of apron, also surrounded by a wall. Below that again, on flatter ground and spreading towards the south, was a third section which was probably unfortified. When the Greeks took over the hillside in 1262 it must have been bare of buildings except for the great castle on the summit and one or two houses lower down, intended for the use of the families of the garrison. In particular, half-way up the slope, where there was a fairly level terrace, the Franks had built a residence of some elegance, looking out eastward over the plain. It was probably here that the castellan lived with his wife and family when his presence was not needed in the castle itself.

The Greeks who came up from Lacedemonia in the years following

1262 to live in the security of Mistra seem at first to have settled in the north-eastern corner of the lower town. It was here that the earliest churches in the city were built. As the governors of the Byzantine province still preferred to live at Monemvasia the foundation of churches in Mistra was left to local officials or ecclesiastics. Of these the most remarkable at the end of the thirteenth century was a cleric, Pachomius, who for some time acted as Protosyncellus of the province and was greatly respected for his efficiency and for his learning. In about 1295 he saw to the completion of a church dedicated to the Sts Theodore, the first important church to be built in the city, of which modest foundations had been laid by a Higoumenos Daniel. A few years later Pachomius retired from public life to found a monastery, the Brontochion, of which he became abbot. It incorporated the Church of the Sts Theodore; and in about 1310 he added another church, dedicated to Our Lady Hodeghetria, 'she who shows the way', but usually called the Afthendiko, the Master Church. It was to be the main church of the monastery. The elegance and the sophistication of the building, especially in comparison with the Church of the Sts Theodore, shows that Mistra was now important enough, and Pachomius influential enough, to obtain the services of an up-to-date architect and up-to-date decorators, probably from Constantinople. Certainly Pachomius's connections with Constantinople were close enough for him to obtain for his monastery, from the Emperor Andronicus II, in a series of four Imperial chrysobulls issued between 1312 and 1322, wide estates all over the Byzantine province, together with authority over a number of smaller monasteries. Further lands were added by the governor, Andronicus Asen; and in 1375 a number of local notables joined together to give it another large estate. Pachomius also persuaded the Emperor to remove his monastery from the jurisdiction of the local ecclesiastical authorities and place it directly under the Patriarchate of Constantinople: which gave it virtual independence.

It is a further tribute to Pachomius that he seems to have achieved the advancement of his monastery without offending the local Metropolitan. The Metropolitanate of Lacedemonia had been in abeyance since the Frankish conquest early in the thirteenth century; and it was not till some years after the cession of Mistra to the Greeks and the subsequent abandonment by the Franks of the city in the plain that it was revived and its seat moved to Mistra. The first holder of the revived see whose name we know was a certain Theodosius, who was Metropolitan in 1272. His main problem seems to have been to defend his rights against his brother of Monemvasia. The Monemvasiot

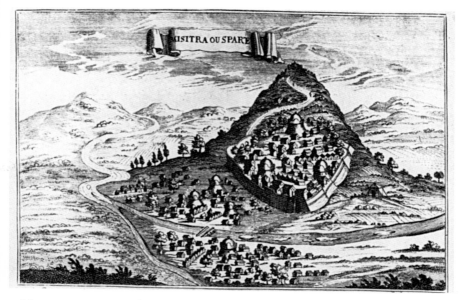

1 Mistra was at one time thought by some to be on the site of the ancient city of Sparta.
Bird's-eye view from V. Coronelli's *Mémoires de la Morée*, 1686

2 Mistra, in an engraving published in 1689, by Bernard Randolph

3 Distant view of Mistra from the theatre of Sparta, by Edward Lear, 1849.

Sparti
March 23 1849 (5)

A broad space or gulf between theatre & olives

Theatre, gray & ocra stone (flat)
faced, on the redder rock — x.

green grass at x x

The whole dark in shade off mountains & plain

The conical hill is separated by precipices from the main Taygetus range

4 The identification of Mistra with Sparta still persists in this engraving, entitled 'Part of Misitra. The Ancient Sparta', by H. W. Williams from a sketch by C. R. Cockerell published in *Sketches in Greece*, 1829

5 Manuel II Palaeologus, from a copy of the funeral oration delivered by him on the death (1407) of his brother Theodore, Despot of the Morea

6, 8, 9 Some of the finest
of Mistra's frescoes are to
be found in the Church
of the Peribleptos: (*left*)
the Nativity; (*bottom left*)
the Denial of Peter;
(*right*) the Descent from
the Cross

7 Soldier saint in cavalry
uniform, from the monastery
of the Brontochion

10 The Preparation of the Throne, from the Metropolitan Church (St Demetrius)

11 The castle dominates the hill of Mistra. In the middle distance is the Pantanassa and in
the foreground the remains of a fountain from the Turkish period

12 South side of the Church of the
Evanghelistria, showing annexed buildings

13 The Pantanassa (*right*)

14 The Palace of the Despots

15 The Church of the Sts Theodore, restored in 1932

16 The Hodeghetria or Afthendiko, built by Abbot Pachomius at the beginning of the fourteenth century

17 The Metropolitan Church seen from the Evanghelistria

Mistra.
2. P.M. 24. *March 1849*

18 The Church of the Peribleptos, drawn by Edward Lear. The original buildings of the monastery that have survived are the tower-like refectory on the left and the church with its chapels to the right

19, 20, 21 Nineteenth-century impressions of: (*top*) the Peribleptos refectory; (*middle*) the Pantanassa; (*bottom*) the setting of Mistra

22 The Peribleptos from the east end, drawn by W. Timson in 1839 (*right*)

23 Another of Lear's sketches of Mistra, showing the Pantanassa with its impressive bell-tower (*below*)

A. D. Aloe)   Mistra.

March   1849

Ἰμπραΐμ πασά.

IBRAHIM-PASHA.

24 Ibrahim Pasha, whose brutality in the Peloponnese shocked Europe and precipitated the intervention of the Great Powers in the Greek War of Independence

Metropolitanate had been revived in 1262, when the Greeks took over the city and it became the residence of the governor of the province. Its holder was raised to a high rank in the episcopal lists and in the later years of the thirteenth century was Exarch, or Patriarchal representative, for the whole Peloponnese. This gave him the right, he considered, to exercise authority over bishoprics that traditionally belonged to Lacedemonia. The dispute centred round the bishopric of Amyclae. When Mistra became the definite capital of the province, its Metropolitan reasonably expected to be the chief ecclesiastic in the province. The Patriarchate solved the problem by appointing to Mistra, or Lacedemonia, some high-ranking prelate whose official see was in the hands of heretics or infidels and who therefore was free to act as *proedros*, or administrator, of the see of Lacedemonia. Nicephorus Moschopoulos, who was appointed to Lacedemonia in about 1304, was officially Metropolitan of Crete, and therefore ranked above the Metropolitan of Monemvasia. His successor, Michael, was Metropolitan of Patras, which, like Crete, was in the hands of the Latins. Later we find the *proedros* Luke, who was Metropolitan of Sougdaia in the Crimea; but in his case it seems that he was eventually able to visit his nominal see. He died in the Crimea in 1339. We do not know the title of his successor, Nilus, who was succeeded in 1365 by a Metropolitan of Traianoupolis. It was only after his time, in about 1387, that the title of Metropolitan of Lacedemonia seems to have been revived.

Little is known of these prelates, except for Nicephorus Moschopoulos. He not only showed energy in defeating the territorial ambitions of the Metropolitan of Monemvasia, but he was interested in culture and the arts. One of his first actions was to provide Mistra with a Metropolitan Church, dedicated to St Demetrius. An inscription tells us that he built it with the help of his brother Aaron, who was no doubt a wealthy layman. It was completed in 1309 or 1310, in the reign of the Emperor Andronicus II and his son Michael.* Nicephorus was in touch with intellectual circles in Constantinople and kept up a correspondence with scholars such as Maximus Planudes and Manuel Philes. The historian Pachymer describes him as a revered and honourable man. He seems to have encouraged the

---

* The date on the inscription is somewhat blurred. It is usually read as representing Anno Mundi 6800 (1291/2 AD), but at that date Michael, son of Andronicus, had not yet been co-opted as Emperor. An alternative reading which gives Anno Mundi 6818 seems preferable, especially as evidence suggests that Nicephorus only came to Mistra in 1304.

Abbot Pachomius to make the Brontochion monastery a centre of learning. In 1311 he presented to the monastery a splendid copy of the Gospels, which was probably the work of scribes in Constantinople, and which found its way eventually to the Synodal Library in Moscow. Pachomius, who, like Nicephorus, was admired by the scholars of Constantinople, was already engaged in having manuscripts copied at Mistra. He and Nicephorus were the pioneers in turning Mistra into a cultural centre.

No doubt the two ecclesiastics were supported by the governor, Andronicus Asen, who was himself the friend of scholars. But there is no evidence that he added any important buildings to the city, though it must have been growing all the time. The next important patron of the arts to live there was the Despot Manuel Cantacuzenus. He found the residence of the governors too small for his needs. So he added to the north of the Frankish house a large wing, probably built in stages, which provided him with a number of large halls on the ground level, with apartments for himself and his courtiers on the upper floor. There were two towers, in one of which there was a chapel. The northernmost section had on its east front a roofed colonnade opening on to a terrace with a splendid view over the Eurotas valley. The Despot Manuel also built, a little further up the hill, an elegant church dedicated to St Sophia, the Holy Wisdom of God; and by it he founded a small monastery. While the Church of St Demetrius remained the Metropolitan Church, the cathedral of the city, it seems that St Sophia was the Court Church, used for the ceremonies of the Despotate. It could be reached on foot from the Palace, up a fairly gentle slope, whereas to reach St Demetrius, the Despot and his courtiers would have had to walk in procession through the narrow streets of the crowded lower city.

Under the Palaeologan Despots the Palace was enlarged again. The wing built by Manuel Cantacuzenus continued to be the residence of the princely family; but now, stretching westward at right angles from the north end of the Palace, a large rectangular block was added, measuring roughly 110 by 35 feet, with cellars and store-rooms at ground level, and above them eight unconnected rooms of considerable size, probably used as offices for the Despot's ministers and courtiers. Above that again was a ceremonial chamber occupying the whole area of the block, with eight great windows, embellished by blind Gothic arches, on the south wall and six on the north wall, and higher up the wall round windows, six on the south wall and eight on the north. Between the two central windows on the south there was an apse, to hold the Despot's throne. Round the rest of the hall there was a continuous stone bench built against the wall, on which courtiers and visitors could sit. In its present ruined state the building is bleak and austere, as it has lost the arcade that ran the length of the south wall on two storeys, giving access to the two lower floors; and there is no trace of the internal decoration. The date of the building is unknown. It is tempting to connect it with the visit that the Emperor Manuel paid to Mistra in 1408, during a brief period of tranquillity, or with his longer visit in 1415, though at that time all available funds had to be devoted to the repair of the wall of the Hexamilion. If an emperor were residing in Mistra, his residence should contain a suitable throne-room.

The establishment of a princely court at Mistra induced the local magnates to build themselves houses in the city. Like Constantinople itself, Mistra did not have a special aristocratic quarter. The houses of the rich might be surrounded by the houses of the poor. But whereas in Constantinople there were squares and open spaces, with gardens around the wealthier dwellings, and bye-laws regulated the minimum width of streets, in Mistra the nature of the terrain with its steep slopes and its restricted area obliged the houses to jostle against each other, sometimes so close together that they met over the street, or there might be passageways under individual houses. With so little level ground there could not be open squares or even broad avenues. The only piazza of any size was the natural platform on which the Palace of the Despots was built. The space in front of the Palace was kept open as a ceremonial parade-ground. It covered a wider area than it does today, when the remains of buildings erected by the Turks restrict it to the west and to the south. Under the Despots, when it was empty but for a fountain put up by Manuel Cantacuzenus, it was the regular meeting-place for all branches of Mistra society.

The upper city was not very thickly populated. This was partly because of the steepness of the hill except in the area round the Palace, and partly because water, which was piped into the city from springs on the far side of the mountain, could not be brought higher than the level of the Palace. Houses and monasteries built further up the hill were dependent, as was the castle on the summit, upon cisterns which caught the rain-water. The rainfall at Mistra can be heavy during the winter months; and there never seems to have been a shortage of water there. But it was clearly more convenient to have a regular piped water-supply. The buildings in the upper city clustered round the Palace and were probably occupied by courtiers and officials and by such workshops as catered for the needs of the Palace. There was one imposing private residence to the west of the Palace, on slightly higher ground, which was large enough to be known colloquially as the Palataki, the Little Palace. It consisted of a tower and a single wing, built probably early in the fourteenth century, to which a similar wing with two side wings, to enclose a courtyard, was added towards the end of the century. Apart from the tower, which was richly decorated, the exterior of the building was austere; but the number of chambers, closets and storerooms within show that it must have belonged to some rich and eminent family. No clue of its identity has survived.

To reach the upper city the easiest route was from outside the walls. The main road from the north came up the hill outside the northern wall, and entered the city through the heavily fortified Nauplia Gate, a little higher up than the Palace of the Despots. Higher up on the same side there was a small postern gate. On the south side the city was protected by precipices, and a continuous wall was unnecessary. Between the upper city and the lower city there was only one gate, known as the Monemvasia Gate, as the road from Monemvasia terminated in the lower city. The street that led up to the Monemvasia gate was narrow and easy to block. The upper city could therefore easily be protected from any riots in the lower city or from an enemy that might penetrate into it. Just above the gate there was a handsome house that must have belonged either to some noble family or perhaps to the official in charge of the city, the local equivalent of the Prefect of the City of Constantinople, who would be well placed there to superintend the citizens.

The northern part of the lower city must have been full of small houses and shops, built close against each other along winding lanes that were often steep and sometimes stepped. The southern quarters were, it seems, less crowded. Here the magnates' houses had room for terraced gardens. Near the bottom of the slope, not far from the eastern wall, a fine mansion, traditionally supposed to have belonged to the Lascaris family, juts out from the hillside. At the east end, over huge vaulted chambers, used for stores and, perhaps, stables, there were two floors, one for servants and offices, and an upper floor which opened on to an elegant balcony looking out over the valley below. At the west end of the building this top floor was on ground level. The little Church of St Christopher, about a hundred yards below the house, was probably the family chapel; and the garden would have stretched down to the lane on which it stands. A little further up the hill there was the house where the great family of the Phrangopouli seem to have lived. It was not so large as the Lascaris mansion, but it jutted similarly out from the hill, with a balcony commanding the view. The lesser buildings are now all so badly ruined that it is impossible to tell which were houses and which were shops. Here and there were fountains from which the poorer citizens could obtain their water. The larger houses had private cisterns into which water was piped.

Foreign merchants seem to have lived in the quarters outside the walls, on the east, where there was also the Jewish colony. It was probably here that the markets were held, as it would have been difficult to drive cattle or sheep through the narrow streets of the walled city.

Indeed, within the walled city, goods could only be carried on the backs of mules or donkeys. Wheeled transport was impossible. In the upper city the Despot and his family could have ridden on horseback out to the countryside through the Nauplia Gate and ladies could have been carried in litters from the Palace to the Church of St Sophia. But in the steep, winding lanes of the lower city neither horses nor litters would have been practicable. The citizens must have gone about their business on foot.

The chief glory of the city was its churches. The secular architecture of Mistra is almost more Western than Byzantine. The greater houses, and the Palace itself, are closer in conception to the smaller old palaces in Italy than to the halls of the Great Palace in Constantinople. But religious architecture remained true to the Byzantine tradition. The only sign of Western influence is in the addition of belfry towers, such as those that grace St Sophia or the Pantanassa. Few of Mistra's churches survive to this day; but most of those that have perished were small chapels which, like the Church of St Christopher, served the family and dependents of some magnate. The tactfully restored Church of St George, in the south-eastern corner of the lower city, is probably typical of them. It is a rectangular building with a barrel-vaulted ceiling, and an apse fitted on to the east end. As the hill rises steeply to the west, the narthex is attached to the south side. The small chapel built beside the lane leading from the Palace to St Sophia is of almost identical design, though its fine frescoes, now barely visible, suggest that it was decorated by one of the Despot's painters. The larger churches were built on terraces cleared for the purpose, but even so were restricted for space.

Architecturally the churches of Mistra are of no regular pattern but follow various past Byzantine styles. The little Church of the Sts Theodore is of the Greek cross style, a small version of the church at Daphni in Attica. Abbot Pachomius's Hodeghetria and Archbishop Nicephorus's Metropolitan Church are domed basilicas, small versions of the Church of St Irene in Constantinople. The Despot

Manuel's St Sophia and the Church of the Evanghelistria in the lower town, of whose history nothing is known, are of the type usually called cruciform distyle, half-way between the Greek cross and the domed basilica, a type to which many Byzantine churches of the Palaeologan age belong. Of the two important later churches, that of the Peribleptos, at the south-east of the lower city, founded by a noble family whose name is unknown to us, is of a similar design, but adapted to fit the rocky configuration of the site: while the Pantanassa, founded in the year 1426 by the Phrangopoulos family, whose head, Manuel, was then chief minister to the young Despot Theodore II, is a basilica. One has the impression that architecture was not of great interest to the cultured circles of Mistra. What appealed to them was decoration. On the exterior, the brick revetment shows a great variety of patterns enlivened by dog-tooth bands, by festoons, by recesses and blind arcades. The interiors were covered with frescoes.

In the impoverished and melancholy city of Constantinople scarcely any new buildings were erected after the middle of the fourteenth century. The repair of the apse of St Sophia after an earthquake in 1346 was the last recorded great artistic undertaking in the capital. We know of frescoes being added to the Church of Our Lady of Sure Hope in the latter half of the century and of more work done to the Church of Our Saviour in Chora. But when one of the holiest shrines of Constantinople, Our Lady of Blachernae, was damaged by fire in 1434, there was neither the money nor, perhaps, the will to repair it. The painters of Byzantium had gone long since to find patrons elsewhere. Work of high quality was still being done in the Empire of Trebizond till well into the fifteenth century. Other painters went from Constantinople to Mistra.

The earliest surviving frescoes of Mistra, those in the Church of the Sts Theodore, are too badly damaged for us to judge of them. But it is clear that Archbishop Nicephorus and Abbot Pachomius both employed artists of a high quality for their Metropolitan and Hodeghetria churches. In the Metropolitan Church many of the upper frescoes were destroyed when a later Metropolitan, Matthew, decided to repair and alter the roof, and many other of the original paintings were covered by later work or by plaster. But enough has now been uncovered to show that the artists must have come from Constantinople and have belonged to the same school that produced that great masterpiece of Byzantine painting, *The Harrowing of Hell*, in the side chapel of the Church of Our Saviour in Chora in Constantinople. It was almost certainly the same group of artists who decorated the contemporary Church of the Afthendiko, the Hodeghetria; and here the frescoes are in a better condition. The workmanship is excellent. The drawing is good. There is a touch of humanity, of human drama and human pathos, about the figures, though their dignity is unimpaired. There is a strong sense of movement. The colours are rich but not too lavish, with something of the disregard for realism that originated with the painters of Trebizond. The pictures perhaps lack the classical restraint that characterized the Master of the Chora; but the artists are worthy to be considered as his colleagues.

The frescoes in the Church of the Peribleptos seem to have been executed about half a century later. It would be interesting to know whether the artists who worked there came out specially from Constantinople for the purpose, or whether they belonged to a local school which had been set up by the artists who had worked for Archbishop Nicephorus and Abbot Pachomius. Unfortunately there are no frescoes of the period surviving in Constantinople that can guide us; and those in the Despot Manuel's Church of St Sophia, for which he must have employed the best available artists, have been so badly spoilt by overpainting and then by coats of plaster when the church became a mosque, that they can provide no useful testimony. In default of further evidence, it is tempting to see the frescoes of the Peribleptos as the work of a native school, as they have an individuality of their own. They belong to the tradition of the frescoes in the Chora. The drawing is still excellent, though the artists now like to soften outlines by subtler gradations in colour. There is still an austere dignity in many of the figures, but here and there a touch of wistfulness comes in. There is a slight loss of vigour. People seem not so much to move as to float. Nevertheless, the decoration of the Peribleptos is the most interesting and successful of all those in Mistra. Some of the individual scenes, such as that of the Divine Liturgy in the north apse, which is unfortunately the darkest corner of the church, or the Nativity in the south transept, are among the greatest of Byzantine works of art.

The Church of the Pantanassa, built in 1428, shows in its decoration how taste had changed in the intervening half-century. The artists were still highly accomplished, with a use of colour that is almost riotous in its variety and its disregard of reality; but the drawing is hampered by a desire to fit too many figures into the space. Somehow the religious intensity of earlier Byzantine work is gone. It is almost as if we were looking at the illustrations to a book of fairy stories. One feels that the artists were trying to transfer a style suited to book-illumination to larger spaces for which it was unsuitable. There is great charm about it all; but it is the art of a civilization that has outlived its political basis, an art of wistful nostalgia for which there was no future. The paintings in the Pantanassa at Mistra formed the last important monument of the medieval free Greek world.

X The Philosophers of Mistra

LONG BEFORE the end of the fourteenth century it was clear that the free Greek world was doomed. By the year 1400 the majority of Greeks lived in the dominions of the Ottoman Sultan, and many others, especially in the islands, were under the government of the Venetians or of local Italian lords. The Emperor ruled over a small and dwindling domain; and in Constantinople the population was impoverished and declining in numbers. Yet never before had the Imperial city been so full of distinguished scholars, theologians, historians and scientists. It remained an intellectual centre which attracted not only all Greek men of learning but also Italians, eager now to study the old Greek lore that Byzantium had guarded down the centuries. But Contantinople was not the only cultural centre for the Greeks. Till the Zealot revolution in the middle of the fourteenth century, Thessalonica was equally renowned for scholarship. Far away in the east the Empire of Trebizond had its own schools, noted for the study of mathematics and astronomy: though many of its scholars drifted to Constantinople. And at the close of the fourteenth century Mistra emerged as a cultural capital. Not only had it already attracted many of the best artists from Constantinople, but now it became a haven for scholarship.

This was due to a hazard. Mistra had had eminent intellectual residents such as the Metropolitan Nicephorus Moschopoulos and the Abbot Pachomius, who were in touch with scholarly friends in Constantinople. About the middle of the fourteenth century the scholar Demetrius Cydones wrote a letter to a friend called George – probably his cousin George Cydones – who decided to settle and study in Mistra. Under the enlightened Despots, Manuel and Matthew Cantacuzenus, scholars were certainly welcome there; and the frequent visits of their father, the ex-Emperor John Cantacuzenus, one of the most erudite men of his time, added to the intellectual prestige of the city. But what brought to Mistra international renown amongst scholars was the arrival there early in the fifteenth century of the most remarkable and original of all Byzantine thinkers, George Gemistus Plethon.

George Gemistus, who took the name of Plethon because it had the same meaning of 'fullness' as his family surname but also echoed the name of his idol, Plato, was born in Constantinople some time in the early 1360s. He came of a scholarly family; his father was a high official at the Patriarchate. He was a brilliant student; but when he had finished his schooling in Constantinople he shocked his compatriots by going off to Adrianople, then the European capital of the Ottoman Sultanate. There he studied for several years under a Jew called Elisaeus. Elisaeus was not only learned in the Aristotelianism of Averrhoes and in Jewish Kabbalistic lore but was also an authority on Zoroastrianism, a subject which fascinated Plethon. Plethon remained for some years in Adrianople, till Elisaeus met his death by burning—probably accidentally as the Turks never employed burning at the stake as a punishment; but to Orthodox onlookers it seemed very appropriate that a Zoroastrian sympathizer should perish through the element of fire. Plethon then returned to Constantinople and began to lecture on philosophy at the University. His knowledge of Aristotelianism was immense, but he rejected it in favour of Platonism. The Church authorities in Constantinople had always been nervous of teachers of Platonism, deeply though Plato's doctrines had penetrated into Orthodox theology. They feared that it might lead to a neo-Platonic polytheism; and in the case of Plethon their fears were not unjustified. There were protests about his lectures and perhaps hints of a prosecution for heresy. Eventually the Emperor Manuel, who was a personal friend of Plethon's and who combined genuine piety with a wise and kindly tolerance, suggested to him that it might be prudent if he moved from the capital to Mistra.

The date was about 1407; for it seems that Plethon was still teaching in the capital in 1405. It was an appropriate moment. Manuel had just sent his second son Theodore, the most scholarly of his children, to take over the rule of the Peloponnese from his dying brother, Theodore I, and he himself was about to pay a long visit there to establish the young Despot's government. Plethon's transfer there could be seen as a tribute to his connection with the Imperial family. He could act as a teacher and adviser to Theodore II.

The move did not distress Plethon, who was delighted to find himself living in a city close to one of the chief historic centres of ancient Greece. For many centuries since the days of Constantine the Great the word 'Hellene' had lost its true meaning. It had been used to denote not a Greek but someone who followed the religion of ancient Greece, a pagan as opposed to a Christian. The citizens of Byzantium in its great days called themselves Roman. They might talk to each other in Greek. Their education might be wholly Greek. But they knew that they were heirs of the Roman Empire. The Empire, however, was dying. In the fourteenth century many of the scholars of Byzantium, conscious of the political decay of their world, and conscious, too, that their one great asset was that Byzantium had preserved unadulterated the learning and literature of ancient Greece, an asset for which they were envied by the scholars of the West, began to revive the word 'Hellene'. They called themselves Hellenes, not in the intention of repudiating their Christian faith but to show that they were the inheritors of classical Greek civilization. Plethon was brought up in this new tradition, and he carried it further. A Hellene, he thought, should live in Hellas, not in New Rome, which was Constantinople. Moreover, as a disciple of Plato, he shared Plato's disapproval of the democratic constitution of ancient Athens, to which, he thought, the political decline of Athens could be directly attributed. He preferred the disciplined tradition of Sparta. His political hero was Lycurgus; and now he was living and teaching close to the very spot where Lycurgus lived and taught.

Apart from a year spent in Italy, in 1438–9, Plethon spent the rest of his life in Mistra. He died there on 26 June 1452, at about the age of ninety. In 1427 the Despot Theodore II bestowed on him some landed property, a village in Argolis and one in Laconia, gifts that were confirmed by later official acts. Indeed, the last decree issued by Constantine XI before he left Mistra for Constantinople was to provide that Plethon's sons, Demetrius and Andronicus, should inherit these properties on his death. But it is highly doubtful if Plethon himself ever lived on his lands. He was a member of the Senate at Mistra and had a high magisterial office there. It is impossible to know where his house was in Mistra; but we picture him, as a philosopher in the old peripatetic tradition, strolling to and fro with his pupils in the great square outside the Despot's Palace, the only level open space in that crowded mountain city.

There, under the friendly patronage of the Imperial family and far away from the ecclesiastical authorities of the Patriarchate, Plethon could air his views with some freedom. But he was prudent enough not to publish his writings on philosophy, in which his doctrines might have seemed too pagan even for his patrons. His most popular work, to judge from the number of manuscripts that survived, was his short obituary encomium of the Despoena Cleope. Its success was, perhaps, as much a tribute to her popularity as to his eloquence. He himself set most store by his political proposals, set forth in two long memoranda addressed to the Emperor Manuel and to the Despot Theodore II. In them he showed how, in his opinion, a strong Hellenic state could still be created in the Peloponnese. It was almost an island and therefore adapted to a bold constitutional experiment. It was also, he claimed with more patriotism than historical accuracy, a land which the same Hellenic stock had always inhabited, from the earliest times, without later immigration, and which the Hellenes had always regarded as being particularly their own.

Plethon's political ideas were based upon Plato's; but he aimed at being practical and up-to-date. He was appalled by the lawlessness of the local lords and their usual oppression of the poor. There should be a strong centralized monarchy. The Despot should have full sovereign powers, but he should be advised by a Council of men drawn from all ranks of society, chosen for their sagacity, their temperance and their dedication. They should be of moderate means. Beneath them, society would be divided into two classes. There would be the soldiers, all of Greek stock, as foreign mercenaries were not to be trusted, enjoying good wages and paying no taxes. Then there would be the tax-payers – merchants, farmers and peasants – from whose taxes, all paid in kind, the military class would be supported. Land-owning was to be abolished. All land would belong to the State; but every farmer and peasant was to be allowed to cultivate just as much land as he and his family could manage, sending a third of his produce to be sold for the benefit of the government. He could build on it and grow what crops he wished. Special encouragement was to be given to those who brought waste land into cultivation. The currency must be reformed; and there would be strict controls upon imports and exports. There must also be penal reforms. Mutilation should be abolished, but the death penalty should be retained; and in a later work he demands that anyone guilty of sexual aberration or misconduct should be burnt at the stake. He seems to have condoned slavery. The Despot and his ministers were to be allowed a limited number of helots. He disapproved of monasticism as making no contribution to the common good.

Plethon saw that, in his own words, 'political recovery is dependent upon constitutional reform'. But his suggested reforms, which were full of ambiguity and at times contradiction, were quite unworkable. No ruler could have forced them on the Peloponnese at that time. We must admire his originality and courage; but a national socialist dictatorship such as he envisaged would rightly have been repugnant to most of the Greeks. The Emperor and the Despot, while they remained devoted to their philosopher–friend, paid little attention to his advice.

His religious views were even more repugnant to contemporary Greek thought. Towards the end of his long life, Plethon completed a book which he called *On the Laws*, and which he had been writing for many years. It is a curious work of which only fragments survive and about which commentators have argued ever since his day. We have his list of contents. His aim was to provide a moral and philosophical background to his political ideas. This led him to propose what was in fact a new synthetic religion, based, he claimed, on the purest Hellenic tradition, in particular on the teachings of Zoroaster, whom he seems to have regarded as an honorary Greek, of Pythagoras and of Plato; and he quotes many other sages of antiquity as his authorities, including King Minos, King Numa of Rome and the Brahmins of India. In fact, all that he knew of Zoroastrianism was the apocryphal *Logia*, or *Oracles*; and his Platonism owes more to the neo–Platonists than to the Master. Of the other sages he knew almost nothing except for their names. In his pantheon are to be found many of the gods of classical Greece, treated as symbols rather than as deities and all united in the supreme Almighty, whom he calls Zeus. Mankind is the link between the gods and the irrational beasts and must therefore stress its rationality and at the same time see that the life cycle continues. The work contains a number of liturgical hymns and prayers to be offered to the gods, and concludes with a fierce attack on the 'sophists', by whom Plethon means the theologians of the Orthodox Church.

It was perhaps natural that Plethon did not venture to publish such a work. When he died in 1452 the manuscript fell into the hands of the Despot Demetrius, who was reigning in Mistra. He did not know what to do with it; but his wife, the Despoena Theodora, read it and felt that she must report on it to her old friend, the philosopher George Scholarius, who had become in 1453, under the name of Gennadius, Patriarch of Constantinople under the Sultan. When he heard of its contents he wrote to the Despoena telling her to destroy it. She was unwilling to take the responsibility, perhaps because Plethon too had been her friend. Indeed, almost his last work had been to write her a charming letter of condolence on the death of her mother-in-law, the Empress Helena. She did nothing; but when she and Demetrius were ejected from Mistra by the conquering Sultan they took the manuscript with them to Constantinople and gave it to the Patriarch. He read it with growing horror and then, before witnesses, consigned the greater part of it to the flames. In his account of the affair one senses that he felt a little guilty at so doing. He also had been a friend of Plethon in the past, though they had had a bitter controversy over the respective merits of Plato and Aristotle. But it would have been impossible in those days for a Patriarch to allow so heterodox a book to be read by the faithful. Other philosophers, Matthew Camariotes and George of Trebizond, were equally horrified by its doctrines. We may regret the Patriarchal action; but it should not surprise us.

It was not by his neo-paganism that Plethon was to enlighten posterity but, indirectly, by his championship of Orthodoxy. It seems certain that there was a neo-paganist cell at Mistra which he dominated and encouraged. In 1450 a Peloponnesian local governor, Manuel Raoul Oises, arrested an itinerant scholar called Juvenal. After a hearing, Juvenal was condemned to have his limbs broken and to be cast into the sea. Such fierce punishments were rare in Byzantium and were only meted out to heretics who were considered to be dangerous to the State. The details of Juvenal's case are obscure. The only surviving evidence comes from the letter written by George Scholarius, then Chief Judge at Constantinople, in reply to the report sent to him by Oises. Juvenal had clearly embarrassed the Imperial family by claiming to be a bastard son of the Emperor Andronicus, Manuel II's eldest brother. The Emperor John VIII exiled him from Constantinople at the request of the local hierarchy, and later from Aenos, where he had taken refuge. So he moved to the Peloponnese, where he had studied in earlier days. There he managed to shock and offend Oises and so met his terrible fate.

Juvenal was probably a half-crazy old man whose indiscretions proved his ruin. But Scholarius clearly believed that it was at Mistra that he had learned his pagan doctrines. Further evidence of the neo-paganist cell is provided by Demetrius Raoul Kavakes, a second-rate scholar who later, when in Italy, edited a work by Julian the Apostate on the Sun-God, which, he said, he greatly regretted that his master Plethon had not known and utilized. He himself, he tells us, had worshipped the Sun-God since the age of sixteen. Plethon's own sons seem to have followed the neo-pagan cult, to judge from the letter of condolence sent them by Bessarion on their father's death, which is worded in neo-Platonic terms and in which Bessarion declares how much he owed to the Master. Bessarion had been by then for fifteen years a cardinal of the Roman Church. We cannot now tell whether his phrases were simply due to a broadminded courtesy or whether he remained faithful in secret to his master's teaching.

Plethon's neo-paganism had no future in the Hellenic world that he so much loved. With the Ottoman conquest the Greeks could only preserve their identity by remaining steadfastly faithful to the Orthodox Church. When Matthew Camariotes, Grand Orator of the Patriarchate after the conquest, published a long attack on Plethon and his teachings, he was flogging a dead horse. Even in Italy the neo-paganism of Mistra had little lasting effect. Its only eminent exponent was the Greco-Italian writer Michael Marullus Tarchaniotes, whom Ronsard called 'that most excellent Greek captain and poet'. It was by his personal influence as a teacher and exponent of Platonism that Plethon was to enrich the civilized world.

Plethon's presence certainly brought scholars to Mistra. Already in 1409, at a ceremony which Plethon attended, a young Peloponnesian ecclesiastic called Isidore was chosen to read out the eulogy written by the Emperor Manuel on his brother, the Despot Theodore I. Isidore remained at Mistra, as Plethon's pupil, till in 1413 he was appointed Metropolitan of Monemvasia. Seventeen years later he was elevated to be Metropolitan of Kiev and head of the Church of Russia. He was a prolific writer during his years in the Peloponnese. Like Plethon he was devoted to the Despoena Cleope. George Scholarius paid more than one visit to Mistra, probably during the 1430s. At that time he was on friendly terms with Plethon; and though they doubtless argued about the respective merits of Plato and Aristotle, there was as yet no acrimony in their dispute. Plethon's most loyal and distinguished pupil was Bessarion of Trebizond. He went to Constantinople as a young man to study at the University and came to Mistra in 1431, where he was attached to one of the monasteries. He spent six years there, sitting at the feet of Plethon, whom he always regarded as his chief master. Aware though he was of Plethon's paganism, he remained officially a staunch Christian. When he eventually retired to Italy he made it one of his eager tasks to temper the scholasticism of Roman theology with something of the Platonism that he had learnt to admire in Mistra. One of the most attractive of Plethon's learned friends was John Eugenicus, younger brother of Mark, Metropolitan of Ephesus, who was the leading opponent during his lifetime of union with Rome. John shared his brother's views on union, but, like Bessarion, he combined a devotion to Platonism with a loyal adherence to Christianity. There were other scholars of lesser renown who sat at the Master's feet. There were Charitonymus Hermonymus and George the Monk, both of them authors of obituary tributes to Plethon. There were the bibliophil John Dokeianus and the learned Nicephorus Cheilas, known as 'the Prince'. There was John Moschus, who succeeded Plethon as the leading resident philosopher.

As the chief luminary in this galaxy of scholars, Plethon became a figure of international repute. In Italy, where the learned world had come to realize what a store of knowledge was to be found in Byzantium, the intellectuals longed to see this illustrious philosopher. Their opportunity came in the early spring of 1438, when Plethon arrived at Ferrara with the delegation led by the Emperor John VIII to discuss and if possible achieve the union of the Orthodox and Roman Churches. It seems at first sight surprising that the Emperor should have chosen a man already suspected of heterodoxy to join the delegation. But John was anxious that the leading philosophers of the Greek world, as well as its clerics, should take part in the discussions. He therefore invited Scholarius, who was still a layman, to represent the philosophers of Constantinople, George Amiroutzes to represent those of Trebizond, and Plethon those of the Peloponnese. For Plethon the chance of visiting Italy was far too attractive for him to allow any philosophical scruples to stand in his way.

At Ferrara Plethon made friends with several Italians. He dined with Cardinal Cesarini and met Francesco Filelfo in the neighbouring city of Bologna. But it was when the Council moved to Florence that he began to enjoy himself. He did not entirely neglect the Council, where he occasionally intervened in support of the Greek point of view; and he was distressed by its outcome. He probably did not add his signature to the Decree of Union, and he certainly arranged to leave Florence, along with the Emperor's brother, the Despot Demetrius, who equally disliked the union, before the final ceremonies took place. But in the meantime he had given a number of lectures on Plato to entranced audiences. However much he disliked Italian theology, he found the Florentine scholars wonderfully receptive, and he basked in their admiration. The actual introduction of Platonic studies into Italian academies was due more to Plethon's disciples, such as Bessarion and John Argyropoulos than to Plethon himself. But he was recognized as the pioneer. When Marsiglio Ficino published his translation of the Enneads of Plotinus a few years later, his introduction contained a tribute to Plethon, 'the second Plato'. It was in Plethon's honour that Cosimo de' Medici founded the Academy at Florence.

Before returning to Mistra Plethon paid a visit to Filelfo at Bologna. He left behind him in Italy a very high reputation. Italian scholars came to see him in Greece. Cyriacus of Ancona, who may be considered the founder of classical archaeology in the West, twice visited him at Mistra. Unfortunately for us, Cyriacus, while he was delighted to find himself close to the site of ancient Sparta, was not in the least interested in contemporary Mistra.

In 1465, a few years after Plethon's death, a Venetian army under the command of the cultured condottiere, Sigismondo Pandolfo Malatesta of Rimini, penetrated into Mistra; and when he was forced to retreat Malatesta took the body of the famous scholar with him from the simple tomb in which it lay and placed it in a noble sepulchre in Rimini. There an inscription pays tribute to 'the greatest philosopher of his time'. The bright light of Mistra where he had shone supremely by then was extinguished. It was fitting that his bones should rest in Italy, the country to which he had helped to bring the Renaissance.

XI The Rule of the Infidel

DEPRIVED of its Despots and of the scholars that thronged their court, Mistra settled down to be a provincial capital within the vast Ottoman Empire. Most of the great Peloponnesian families, such as the Phrangopouli or the Raouli, or Rhallis, who had maintained residences in Mistra, followed their princes into exile, preferring for the most part to live in one of the colonies that Venice still held in Greece, Methone or in Nauplia, or, especially, in Corfu. The smaller landowners remained on their country estates and seldom came to the city. But Mistra was still full of merchants and shopkeepers. It was the headquarters of the silk industry of the vale of Sparta, which the Turkish authorities encouraged. Till 1540 it was the favourite residence of the Pasha who governed the *sandjak*, or province, of the Peloponnese, though he also resided from time to time in Corinth or in Leontarion. In 1540, with the Ottoman capture to Nauplia, that became the Pasha's capital. But a reorganization in 1574, when Venice had lost her last mainland Greek possessions, divided the Peloponnese into two *sandjaks*, one based on Patras and the other on Mistra.

The Turks seem to have taken over the upper city. The Pasha lived in the old Palace of the Despots. The Palace Church of St Sophia was transformed into a mosque. In the castle on the summit of the hill there was now a large Turkish garrison, with a house for the military commander and, probably, a small mosque. In the lower city the Greeks lived on undisturbed. The sprawling suburb outside the walls was still largely occupied by foreign merchants. There had been a small Jewish colony there under the Despots. Under the Turks this colony was greatly increased.

In many parts of the Peloponnese, as in Central Greece, the Sultan distributed fiefs to his veteran warriors. The holder of a larger fief, a *zaimet*, was required to provide fifteen fully-equipped horsemen for the Sultan's army. The holder of a *timar* only had to provide two. But no such fiefs were set up in the countryside round Mistra. Later travellers noted that the population in the vale of Sparta was purely Greek. The Peloponnesian towns were allowed to keep their municipal self-government. Very few Turks lived in them, apart from the garrisons of the fortresses and a handful of officials in the administrative centres. So long as order was kept and the taxes were paid, the Turkish authorities did not interfere. Taxation, based on a capitation tax, was in general lower than it had been under the Despots; and each town had the right to send two elected officials, known as 'primates', every year to Constantinople to report to the Sultan any illegal exaction or persecution instigated by the local governors. In addition, each subdivision of the province could send two delegates chosen from its leading citizens, once or twice a year, to discuss local affairs with the Pasha. For the administration of justice the Greeks had their own courts, managed by the municipality under the authority of the Church. Only when a Muslim was involved did the case have to go before the Muslim judge, the *cadi*. There was a *cadi* resident in each of the major cities. The Church retained its old privileges. Priests were officially freed from the duty of paying taxes. But, in fact, the local bishops found it advisable now and then to give handsome presents to the Pasha and his officials, particularly when church appointments had to be confirmed by the Turkish authorities.

All in all, the Greeks of the Peloponnese did not fare too badly under Turkish rule, at least till the close of the sixteenth century, when the Turkish government was still conducted with efficiency and tolerance. But they were desperately conscious of being second-class citizens under an infidel power; and they had two specific grievances. The Turks firmly discouraged the setting up of Christian schools. A child of a merchant or a richer shopkeeper would be given a basic education; but a clever boy who wanted a higher education would have to go to Constantinople, where the Patriarchal Academy was still allowed to function, or, better, would have to make his way to a Venetian colony and thence to Venice, where the rich Greek colony would look after him and, if possible, send him to study at the University of Padua. There, uniquely amongst Italian universities, no attempt was made to seduce him from his Orthodox faith. For the peasants in the countryside no education was now available. The monasteries which had supplied simple schooling in the past were now themselves increasingly filled with illiterate monks. Even the abbots and bishops were unable to spell correctly.

The second cause of resentment was the child tax, the *paidomazoma*, as the Greeks called it, by which the Sultan's élite corps of Janissaries was recruited. Every five years, and sometimes more often, a Turkish officer would descend on towns and villages and demand from the headman a list of the Christian families and of their children. The fathers would then produce their sons for inspection; and the officer would choose those that seemed strongest or most intelligent. The boys were then taken to Constantinople and forcibly converted to Islam. Once they entered the corps, which provided the Sultan with his engineers and technicians as well as his soldiers, they were forbidden to marry but had to devote themselves entirely to the service of the State. At first the boys were taken at the age of six or seven, only one from each family, never an only son, and only one in five of the eligible boys of the district. In the sixteenth century these rules were abandoned. An arbitrary proportion of boys might be taken, and the boys might be in their teens. It was only in the later seventeenth century, when the Janissaries were allowed to marry and so turned the corps into a hereditary body, that the child-tax faded out. The Peloponnese seems to have suffered a little less than many Christian areas from the depredations of the tax. It is remarkable that only one revolt caused by it is recorded; and that was organized by Christian Albanians in 1565. Some Christian parents were rumoured to welcome the tax, as a Janissary could rise to riches and to power, and often, especially if he had been recruited in his teens, he kept in touch with his relatives and was able to help them in many ways. There were even said to be Muslim families that pretended to be Christian in order to have the asset of a Janissary son. But the Christian communities in general could not but suffer from the loss of so many of their ablest boys.

The best that could be said of Ottoman rule was that it brought comparative peace and order to a province that for the last centuries had been troubled by ceaseless wars. The peace was not unbroken. There were wars between the Turks and the Venetians that were waged on and off from 1463 to 1479. In the course of them Venice lost Argos but acquired, at the wish of its citizens, the great fortress of Monemvasia. There was war again from 1499 to 1503, when Venice lost all her Peloponnesian possessions except for Nauplia and Monemvasia, and from 1537 to 1540, when in a shameful treaty she ceded those two uncaptured fortresses to the Turks. But these wars were fought mostly at sea, and only the coastal districts were badly affected. In 1465 Sigismondo Malatesta made his expedition to Mistra, during which he removed the body of Plethon.

Thenceforward for more than two centuries Mistra was left in tranquillity. The city enjoyed considerable prosperity. The Turkish authorities there were on the whole efficient and benevolent, if rather contemptuous, towards the Christians. The periodical presence of the Pasha and his entourage in the city stimulated the bazaars. The silk farms in the valley flourished; and foreign merchants came to Mistra to buy their products. The growth of the Jewish colony indicates that Mistra was an important commercial centre. Its inland situation saved it not only from the effects of the Turco-Venetian wars but also from the depredations of the pirates, whose activities in Aegean waters grew more and more destructive in the latter years of the sixteenth century.

There was always a certain risk in the proximity of the Mani. Its inhabitants had never been effectively subdued by the Turks, and they took every opportunity of rising against them and seeking to involve their neighbours. At other times they were delighted to ravage their neighbours' richer territory. The citizens of Mistra often had cause to be grateful for their Turkish garrison. To quote the words of an English traveller, Bernard Randolph, who visited Mistra in 1671 and describes it as the biggest city in the Peloponnese after Patras, 'Tho' this City stands remote from the Sea, and free from dangers, from thence, yet the Manjotts are a People apt to prey upon them'.

In about 1612 a Franco–Italian noble, Charles Gonzaga of Mantua – who had inherited the Duchy of Nevers from his French mother and whose paternal grandmother had been the last member of the branch of the Imperial line of the Palaeologi who had inherited the Marquisate of Montferrat – decided to claim the throne of Constantinople and sent secret envoys to Greek lands to ask for support. The Maniots received his advances with enthusiasm. Three Maniots went to France to visit the Duke and promised to recognize him as their liege lord if he would send officers to train their soldiers. The Duke's own envoys returned with optimistic stories of the enthusiasm that they had found in the peninsula. The Greeks were ready to adopt Catholicism, they said, if the Duke would drive out the Turks; and the Bishop of Maina gave them a message for the Duke, in which he was addressed as Constantine Palaeologus, even persuading the Metropolitan of Lacedemonia to add his signature to it. However, it is to be doubted whether the Metropolitan, who belonged to the distinguished family of Lascaris, would have accepted the religious suggestion. It was prophesied that within a few months the double-headed eagle of the Palaeologi would be flying over Mistra. The scheme was not entirely wild. It was calculated that the Peloponnese could provide 15,000 fighting-men, whereas the Turks only had 8,000 potential soldiers in the province, most of whom formed the garrisons of the greater fortresses. But the Duke delayed. He was prudent enough not to start on the adventure without solid diplomatic backing; and he hoped to organize risings in other European provinces of the Ottoman Empire. His efforts came to very little. When at last he collected five ships to carry his own soldiers to Greece, they were destroyed by fire, perhaps by saboteurs; and his agents in the Balkans were unable to promise adequate support for him. After some twelve years of fruitless plotting the Duke abandoned his scheme, contenting himself with a claim to his native Dukedom of Mantua. It is probable that the citizens of Mistra, and their Metropolitan, were greatly relieved.

Some twenty years later, when war broke out again between Venice and the Turks in 1645, Mistra was once more threatened by the Maniots. The Venetian commander, Morosini, persuaded them, without difficulty, to raid the neighbouring provinces, while an Albanian rising resulted in the ravaging of the centre and the west of the peninsula. But it seems that Mistra and its immediate neighbourhood escaped the raids; and when the Ottoman Vizier, Ahmed Köprülü, was able to instigate a vendetta between two of the leading families of the Mani, in which the whole district was soon involved, the raids ceased and the rest of the Peloponnese sighed with relief. The long war between Venice and the Turks ended only in 1669, with the Venetian loss of Crete. But the mainland was no longer troubled.

It was shortly after the conclusion of peace that Bernard Randolph visited Mistra and wrote the first account of it that we have from an English traveller. A few years previously a Frenchman, Giraud, and another Englishman, Vernon, had separately been to Mistra but had little to say about it except to note that it was not built upon the site of ancient Sparta, though that was now the local belief. Randolph was not so sure. To him the city is 'Mesitha, formerly called Lacedemon'; and he noted some ruins, including the arch of an aqueduct, adjoining the city below the hill, which he decided must belong to the classical town. He found the vale of Sparta 'very pleasant' and was impressed by its prosperity. But he did not approve of what he considered to be the superstition of its inhabitants and told with relish of a recent Pasha, who, hearing that there was a holy icon of the Virgin in a nearby village which was said to perform miracles, had it and a secular picture brought to him and threw them both on a fire, saying that he would venerate whichever of them survived the flames. Both of them perished. The story is typical of the mocking contempt with which the Muslim authorities all too often treated the simple Christian villagers. But the villagers' faith remained unimpaired.

Sir George Wheler and his French companion, Dr Spon, came to the Peloponnese in 1677, but did not manage to reach Mistra. Giraud, a

Huguenot who acted as English Consul in Athens and had married a Greek wife, assured them that Mistra was not Sparta, while Vernon had reported that there was nothing to be seen on the ancient site. They probably therefore did not think it worth a visit.

In 1684 war broke out again between Venice and the Turks. The Venetians, still smarting from the loss of Crete fifteen years earlier, chose the moment well. In 1683 the Turks had been defeated before Vienna; and both the Habsburg Emperor and John Sobieski, King of Poland, who had commanded the army that relieved the Imperial capital, were eager to follow up their victory. A Holy Alliance, under the patronage of the Pope, was formed between Venice, Austria and Poland. At a conference at Linz, in March 1684, each state swore not to make a separate peace, and each promptly declared war on the Sultan. The Turks were compelled to concentrate their main forces against the Austrian attack; for the Poles, in fact, played only a small part in the war. The Greek peninsula was thus inadequately garrisoned against the Venetians. The Venetian forces were composed mostly of German mercenaries, under their own commanders, of whom Count Königsmarck was the most distinguished. But the supreme command was given to the aged Francesco Morosini, who had been responsible for the long and heroic, though unavailing, defence of Crete against the Turks.

Morosini spent 1685 and 1686 in capturing a number of vital coastal fortresses. Nauplia, at that time the capital of the province, was captured towards the end of 1686. Early the next spring Morosini's troops set about the systematic conquest of the interior of the Peloponnese. There was very little resistance from the Turkish garrisons. Even the almost impregnable fortress of Acrocorinth was surrendered without a struggle. Mistra was one of the last cities to fall into Venetian hands. By August, Venice controlled the whole Peloponnese, with the exception of Monemvasia, which after a long siege was starved into submission in 1690. The grateful Republic bestowed upon Morosini the title of 'Peloponnesiacus'.

The conquest of the Peloponnese marked the limit of Venetian success during the long war. Morosini went on to attack Athens; and on 26 September 1687, a gunner from Lüneburg fired the fatal shot that exploded a powder-magazine which the Turks had placed in the Parthenon. By the end of the month the Turkish garrison had surrendered. But Morosini soon realized that he did not have enough troops against the large Turkish army that was now assembled at Thebes. By March 1688, it was decided to abandon the city. The water-supply had been damaged during the siege; and now plague was making its appearance amongst the troops. Many Athenian families who had welcomed the Venetians and now feared Turkish vengeance left with the army and were given new homes in the Peloponnese, where they received a chilly welcome from the local Greeks. Morosini's further schemes of conquest, which included an invasion of Euboea, came to nothing. He himself retired, a sick old man, to Venice, where he spent the rest of his days as Doge. Meanwhile, there was a revival of Turkish power, under a vigorous new Vizier, Mustafa Köprülü, perhaps the ablest of his able family, who made it his special task to reconcile the Christian minorities under his rule. The war dragged on, with the Turks now recovering ground from the Holy Alliance, till at last a great victory of the Austrians under Eugene of Savoy at Zenta on the River Theiss in September 1697, restored the balance. The belligerents were now ready to accept the mediation of the English. Peace was signed at Carlovitz in January 1699.

By this peace treaty, Venice secured the Ionian Islands, apart from Leucas, Aegina and Tenos in the Aegean, two fortresses in Epirus and two in Crete, and the whole Peloponnese. The Turks had made no attempt to recover the peninsula; and the Venetian administration was well established there.

The Peloponnesians had at first welcomed their new masters. The Turkish administration had become arbitrary and corrupt, with little control from Constantinople. It was a relief to return to Christian rule. The Venetians were Catholics, but they enjoyed a good reputation for religious tolerance. The Greek colony in Venice was prosperous and well regarded, with its own Orthodox Church; and many young Greeks had been educated there and at the University of Padua. Venetian officials were known to be efficient, and Venetian justice fairly administered. But disillusion soon set in. The plague, which had appeared shortly after Morosini's 1687 campaign, swept through the peninsula and the inhabitants blamed the invaders for having introduced it. The Venetian authorities calculated that the population, which had been about 200,000 before the invasion, had sunk by the end of 1688, to under 100,000. Of 2,111 villages 656 lay desolate. Mistra and the vale of Sparta suffered less from the devastation caused by the military and by the plague than did the western districts of the peninsula; but they did not emerge unscathed.

There was soon resentment against the Venetian administration. It was far more competent than the Turkish; but the Turks had at least allowed the towns to be self-governing. Now the Venetian *provveditore* was in complete charge of the municipality. To Mistra this was particularly galling. It was no longer the capital of a province. The province of Laconia had its capital at Monemvasia. But, along with six other secondary towns, it had its own *provveditore*, who, not having also a province to superintend, could devote all his time to interfering in the affairs of the citizens. Moreover, though the Greeks were spared from the periodical necessity to bribe the Turkish authorities, the taxes levied by the Venetians were higher than Turkish taxes had been, and they were efficiently collected. Again, though the Venetians did much to encourage local agriculture and some local industries, they deliberately discouraged any industry that competed with their own in Italy. This fell very hardly upon Mistra, whose prosperity depended largely on the silk farms of the neighbourhood. The heavy duties levied on local silk, in the interests of the silk farmers of the Veneto, raised the price of Spartan silk so high that foreign merchants moved away to buy cheaper silk in Asia Minor.

Finally there was the question of religion. In Venice itself and in the Ionian Islands relations between the Catholics and the Orthodox were not unfriendly. The Venetians were at first eager to show goodwill to the Church of their new subjects. The congregations were confirmed in their right to elect their own bishops, without any political pressure; and only one Catholic see was instituted, the Archbishopric of Corinth, whose titular habitually resided at Nauplia, the Venetian capital. But in the wake of the Venetian officials a number of Catholic priests entered the country, men who, as the Venetian Governor-General, Cornaro, sadly remarked, seemed to have been sent there rather as a punishment for their own sins than to correct the sins of others. Their arrogance towards the native clergy made them hated. But some of them started schools; and to the Greeks, who had been starved of education under the Turks, this provided an opportunity for their sons to be given some learning. Many Greek boys took advantage of this; but their parents were continually angered by the teachers' attempts at religious proselytism.

The main practical religious problem was not, however, the fault of the Venetians. The Orthodox in the Peloponnese owed religious obedience to the Patriarch of Constantinople, who not only confirmed the election of its nineteen bishops and the abbots of its greater monasteries, which were directly dependent on him, but also received one half of the Epiphany and Easter offerings contributed by the congregations. But the Patriarch lived in the shadow of the Sultan and in the oath taken at his election he swore to see that the Christians under his care would be loyal to the Sultan's secular rule. The Venetians not only deprived the Patriarch of his right to confirm episcopal elections, but they saw no reason why good Peloponnesian money should go to an enemy country. There were also churches and monasteries in Ottoman territory, such as the Patriarchate of Jerusalem and some of the Athonite houses, which owned property in the Peloponnese. The Patriarchal Exarch sent to collect the offerings and the rents and to confirm the episcopal elections was refused admission into the country. The pious Peloponnesians showed no gratitude to Venice for their ecclesiastical independence, nor for being allowed to keep the money due to the Patriarchate for use in their own dioceses. Their senior ecclesiastic, the Metropolitan of Patras, did what he could to see that the Patriarch and the other interested churches and monasteries in Ottoman lands received their proper revenues, to the continued annoyance of the Venetian governor. Meanwhile, news reached the Peloponnese of the greatly improved treatment of the Sultan's Christian subjects, due to the influence of the Vizier, Mustafa Köprülü.

Nevertheless, there was no attempt by the Greeks to rise against Venetian rule. The restless Maniots much preferred the Venetians to the Turks, so long as they were not asked to pay taxes. They ceased to raid their landward neighbours, and concentrated their attention on piracy. The other Peloponnesians had lost any taste for fighting. Venetian observers considered them to be suspicious, lazy and jealous of each other. They were, it was thought, less cultured than the Ionians: which was natural, for the Ionians had had a long connection with Venice and possessed their own schools. Men and women of polish could be found in Kalamata; but it was generally agreed that the most civilized city in the province was Mistra. The Venetian author Coronelli, Geographer to the Venetian Republic, published a book on the Peloponnese as it was soon after the Venetian conquest, in which he gave a full description of Mistra. He firmly believed it to be the town 'first called Sparta, then Lacedemon, and now Misitra'; and his account includes a somewhat fanciful history of Sparta, with an incomplete list of its kings, as well as some inaccurate information on the medieval history of the town. But Coronelli's account of it as it was in his own time can be considered reliable. As in the past it was divided into quarters. He treats the castle, 'called *to Castron*', as forming one quarter. Next was the quarter which he calls La Terra, and which the Greeks called Chore, the upper city of Palaeologan times, which, till the Venetians came, contained the residences of the Turks, each of which, he tells us, had to keep a cellar stocked with grain, for the military to use were there a siege. It also contained a large number of cisterns. Below it was the Mesokhorion – he miscalls it Melokorion – the lower city of medieval times and now, as its name implied, the middle city. Outside the walls there was the Exokhorion, separated from the rest by the little River Vasolipotamos, over which there was only one bridge. This outer city must have stretched down to the modern town of Mistra. The Turks called it Maratche.

Other Venetian sources estimate the population of Mistra at the time of the Venetian conquest at about 40,000. Randolph had thought that in the Peloponnese only Patras was larger; but the Venetian capital, Nauplia, probably soon outnumbered each of them.

The Republic's possession of the Peloponnese was short-lived. By 1714 the Turks were ready for revenge. They had recently defeated the Russians and were at peace with all their other neighbours. They had the diplomatic sympathy of France, whose merchants were eager to increase their trade with the Levant at the expense of the Venetians. They knew that the Greeks would do nothing to support their Venetian masters. On the Sultan's demand the Oecumenical Patriarch wrote to urge his bishops to return to their old allegiance. The Republic's former allies, the Habsburg Empire and Poland, would not intervene. She was isolated.

The Sultan declared war at the end of 1714, on the excuse that Venice had been arming the Montenegrans against him. Early the next year a Turkish army of more than 100,000 men marched down to the Isthmus of Corinth, and a great fleet sailed into the Aegean, capturing without a struggle the island of Tenos, which had been Venetian for over three centuries. The Venetians decided to defend only their fortresses by the coast. After a bombardment of five days the commander at Corinth, Minotto, surrendered on honourable terms; but an explosion in the arsenal caused the Turks to doubt his good faith. They massacred the garrison and a number of non-combatant Greeks, while Minotto himself was sent to be sold in the slave-market at Smyrna, where he was bought by the wife of the Dutch Consul. After this example there was little further resistance. Both in the towns and in the countryside the Turks were welcomed as deliverers. Moreover, as a French onlooker, Brue, noted with surprise, the Turkish army, unlike the Venetians, paid for the provisions that it obtained from the peasants. At Nauplia the Greeks in Venetian service left their posts, and no offer of high pay would bring them back. There the Venetian garrison made some resistance. But the Turks had obtained from a Frenchman, De la Salle, who had been an officer in the Venetian army, full plans of the great castle of Palamede, which dominated the city. With their help they stormed the castle and from there poured down into the city. In the massacre that followed few Venetians survived. The dead included the Latin Archbishop.

The fall of Nauplia opened the whole interior of the Peloponnese to the Turks. The Venetians swiftly removed their garrisons from Mistra and the other inland cities; and, after a number of mutinies, even the coastal castles were abandoned. The governor of Monemvasia, Badoer, hastened to surrender his fortress to the Turkish admiral, who admitted that he could never have taken it by storm: while the Venetian admiral carefully avoided any action for fear of providing his country with yet another defeat. By the end of 1715 there were no Venetians left in the peninsula.

The war dragged on for another three years, as Austria became involved in it. At the Treaty of Passarovitz, signed in July 1718, Venice lost all her Greek empire with the exception of the Ionian Islands, including Leucas, and the port of Butrinto, opposite to Corfu. Meanwhile, the Peloponnese sank back into its old life as a province of the Ottoman Empire.

The Venetian episode had not been a happy experience for the Greeks of the Peloponnese. They had been treated as a subject, heretic race, and they had been exploited in the interests of Venetian commerce. But it had created a new spirit amongst the Greeks. The Venetian bureaucracy had been slow and fussy in its operations and expensive to maintain; but it had kept order in the province, it had, however selfishly, aided agriculture and commerce, and it had respected the rights of the individual, such as they were. To return to the easy-going but arbitrary and corrupt government of Ottoman pashas might be a relief, but it could not but seem retrogressive. It also brought a decline in education. For a generation Peloponnesian boys had enjoyed easy access to Venice and its higher schools and the University of Padua; and in the peninsula itself there had been the schools set up by Latin priests, resented for their attempts to proselytize, but nevertheless well patronized. The Turks, when they returned, were not so actively hostile to Christian schools as they had been in the past. But they did not encourage them; and in any case there were few adequately trained native teachers. It was less easy for bright boys to escape to the West. But those that succeeded found a new spirit there, the old values, especially the old religious values, being jettisoned for what was thought to be enlightenment. They came back imbued with ideas of liberty for the Greeks. The Church was not very happy about such ideas. It had welcomed the return of the Turks, not only because it freed their congregations from the proselytizing efforts of Roman missionaries but also because it restored their canonical connections with the Patriarchate of Constantinople. If liberty was to be sought, it should be achieved with Orthodox help. In the seven-

116

teenth century Sir Paul Ricaut had noticed that the one foreign power of which the Greeks spoke with affection was Russia, the one independent Orthodox power. Russia under the Romanov tsars had always shown a sympathetic and charitable interest in her Orthodox brethren; and, as the eighteenth century advanced, her ability to give them practical aid steadily improved. If it were Orthodox Russia that was to help the Greeks in the struggle for freedom, the loyalty of the Oecumenical Patriarch and his flock to the Sultan would no longer be reliable.

In 1768 the Empress Catherine II of Russia declared war upon the Sultan. The war was primarily due to dissidents in Poland seeking to ally themselves with Turkey against the Empress's growing control of their kingdom. But her agents working within the Ottoman Empire had busily emphasized her interest in the welfare of the oppressed Orthodox. Their work found ready audiences in the Aegean Islands and in the Peloponnese. Early in 1770 a large Russian fleet set out from the Baltic under the official command of Alexis Orloff and actually directed by two British-born sailors, Greig and Elphinston. Sailing round through the Straits of Gibraltar it reached Greek waters early in April and anchored off Vitylo, the modern Oitylo. A small Russian force was landed under Alexis Orloff's brother, Fyodor.

The Russians had expected to be greeted by a general rising of the Greeks. Their agents had distributed arms all over the peninsula and reported messages from village headmen telling of their preparations. There was reported to be great indignation because in the previous autumn a party of peasants returning merrily from a fair at Patras had been massacred by the Turks, who mistook them for insurgents. But the indignation had worn off, while the headmen's preparations consisted of what they thought of doing rather than what they had actually done. Nevertheless, the local bishop came to meet the Russians, and with him came the Metropolitan of Lacedemonia, to be followed by a number of fighting-men from Mistra and the neighbouring countryside, while the Maniots were always ready to join an expedition against the Turks. Fyodor Orloff set out at the head of a small Greco–Russian force over the mountains to Mistra. The Turkish garrison in Mistra was small, and it received no reinforcements from the Pasha. After a few days of resistance it surrendered to the Christian army. A general massacre of the Turks was prevented only by the Metropolitan and his clergy, who threatened with excommunication anyone who should harm them, and allowed them to make their way to safety. Meanwhile, their houses, and many Greek houses as well, were thoroughly pillaged by the Russians.

On 27 May (O.S.) 1770, the Empress wrote to her friend Monsieur de Voltaire that the troops of Fyodor Orloff had overrun the Morea. Misistra, which is the ancient Sparta, had, she wrote, offered the strongest resistance. But even by the date that she wrote this triumphant letter, things were not going well in the Peloponnese. It was quite untrue that Fyodor Orloff had overrun the whole province. His little army had not moved beyond Laconia. The Greeks had expected the Russians to provide a larger army and far more arms, as well as money. All that they actually received was not enough for them to venture on a rising. Nor were the Russians wise or tactful in dealing with their would-be allies. At Vitylo there broke out a bitter quarrel between Alexis Orloff and Mavromikhaili, the leading chieftain of the Mani, a man who was not going to take orders from an upstart Russian. The Russian fleet was eager to sail on and meet the Turkish fleet. Meanwhile, the governor of the province was gathering an army of Muslim Albanians from the north with which to suppress the rising. He marched on Mistra. There was a skirmish when he descended into the plain of Sparta. Then the Russians retired to the coast, leaving the Greeks to bear the brunt of Turkish vengeance.

The Russian fleet, with the soldiers on board, sailed away from Vitylo in June, to win a great victory over the Turks off Chios the following month and then to burn the whole Turkish fleet in the Gulf of Cheshme a few days later. But these Christian triumphs were of little avail to the Greeks of Mistra. The Russians had barely left before the Pasha's Albanian troops poured into Mistra.

The sack of the city that ensued was merciless and thorough. Houses were robbed of their contents and then set alight. The Albanians were in no mood to make nice distinctions; and many Turkish houses suffered the fate of their Greek neighbours. Even the castle on the summit of the hill was left as a ruin. The churches were systematically looted. Some were destroyed and some so badly ruined as to be unfit for use; but, happily, none of the finer churches suffered great structural damage. The Metropolitan Church seems to have been the worst treated; and in its courtyard the Pasha put to death the Metropolitan, Ananias Lambardis, on the charge of having welcomed the Russian invaders. He paid no heed to his intervention that had saved so many Turkish lives when the invaders reached Mistra. Many other Greeks perished at the hands of the Albanians; and many Christian children were taken away to be sold into slavery.

By the autumn of 1770 Mistra was a city of ruins. Its monuments and its houses had survived three centuries of infidel rule almost intact. But now its greatness was over and its days were numbered.

XII   The End of Ancient Mistra

FOR NINE YEARS life in the vale of Sparta, and in the whole Peloponnese, was miserable and desolate. The Turkish Pasha who had brought in the Albanians to crush the Greek rising found himself unable to pay them the wages that they demanded. So they threw out their Turkish commanders, broke up into bands and set out to ravage the province. There were some 20,000 of them, well able to do as they pleased with a population that was forbidden to bear arms. Even the Turkish land-owners, to whom arms were permitted, could do nothing against them. The Albanians disliked the Turks as much as they disliked the Greeks.

The Russo-Turkish War had come to an end in 1774, with the Treaty of Kutchuk Kainardji, which gave to the Empress the right, a little vaguely worded, to intervene in the Ottoman Empire on behalf of its Orthodox subjects. But Catherine was no longer interested in the Peloponnese, after the failure of the rising there. 'The Greeks, the Spartiates, are degenerate', she wrote to Voltaire in October 1770; 'They prefer rapine to liberty.' Voltaire replied subserviently, blaming the Russian set-back on the Greeks. The Peloponnesians could not now hope for any help from St Petersburg. The Sultan at Constantinople, however, was gravely worried, if only because he was receiving no revenue from the disturbed province. Between 1770 and 1779 eleven different pashas were sent out to restore order. Of these some reported that they could do nothing without military help; some cowered behind the walls of Tripolitza till their friends at the court could arrange for their transfer to a happier post; some received bribes from the Albanians to leave them to carry on as they pleased. At last in 1779 the Sultan sent out a regiment under his ablest officer, the Kapitan-Pasha Hassan, a former Algerine corsair, who had been the only Ottoman naval officer to emerge with credit out of the Russian War. He was no friend to the Greeks. After the war he was given the task of restoring order in the Aegean Islands. His methods were summary. It was said that 100,000 Greeks there were put to death. But the Greeks of the Peloponnese welcomed him and gave him every assistance.

He and his men arrived at Nauplia in May. He waited for a month at Argos, trying to persuade the various Albanian chieftains to submit to him without a struggle. Their answer was to collect together an army of some 10,000 men for an attack on Tripolitza. When he heard that they were assembled there he marched overnight over the high mountain pass that leads from the Argolid to the Arcadian plain. At dawn on 11 June he fell upon the unsuspecting Albanians. He showed them no mercy. By nightfall most of them were slain; and Hassan had erected outside the eastern gate of Tripolitza a pyramid made of some four thousand skulls, which was still visible twenty years later. The few Albanians that escaped from the battle were pursued by Hassan's men into a narrow valley, where they were all massacred.

There were still numbers of Albanians settled throughout the peninsula, in villages and farms that they had forcibly seized. But they made little further trouble, seeking, rather, to merge into the indigenous population. In any case, few seem to have settled in the vale of Sparta. There, when order was restored, the Greeks with their characteristic resilience recovered much of their old prosperity. After the Albanian sack of the city, the population had dropped to some 8,000 souls. Thirty years later it had risen to a figure between 15,000 and 18,000. A table compiled by Dr Pouqueville in about 1800 shows that the annual value of the produce of Mistra and its district was estimated at 875,000 piastres. This put it far ahead of any other district in the province. The produce of Patras, which came second, was valued at 696,092 piastres. Mistra's prosperity was mainly due to the revival of the local silk-farms.

The last decades of the eighteenth century saw a remarkable increase in the number of Western travellers visiting Greece. There was a growing interest in classical archaeology. In England the Society of Dilettanti financed scholarly expeditions to examine and record classical sites. The French had inherited a more eccentric tradition, stemming from Guillet, who preferred to call himself Le Guilletière, and who published in the 1670s two works entitled *Athens, Ancient and Modern* and *Ancient and Modern Lacedemon*. He had, in fact, visited neither place, as Dr Spon, who was a careful scholar, soon found out, but derived his information from a Capuchin friar at Patras. Then in the 1730s there was the Abbé Fourment, travelling on the orders of Louis XIV to collect inscriptions. He collected a few, but having done so spent the rest of his time trying single-handed to demolish whatever classical site he visited. Amongst other places he went to Sparta and spent six weeks there on his eager work of destruction. His one regret was not to have been able to destroy Olympia. The later French preferred more sentimental works, comparing the glories of the Grecian past with the wretchedness of the modern Greeks. Till about 1790 French travellers predominated. Then the French Revolution, followed by Napoleon's dreams of a Levantine empire, made them no longer welcome in Ottoman lands; and the British took their place. The long war with France interrupted the usual itinerary of the Grand Tour, which was considered part of a British young gentleman's education. But, once Napoleon's invasion of Egypt had ended in failure, it was possible to sail through the Mediterranean to Greece. Lord Byron was only one of many who made the journey. Few of those who recorded their travels visited Mistra; but there must have been many others whose names have not survived. The Vicomte de Chateaubriand, who was in Greece in 1805, after peace had been made between France and Turkey, declared that English travellers were to be seen on every road in the Peloponnese and that at Mistra there was a hostelry called 'The English Inn', which provided roast beef and port for its clients.

Of these French and British travellers the one who tells us most about Mistra is Dr Pouqueville. The circumstances of his journey were unusual. He had gone as an army doctor with the French expedition to Egypt in 1798, but in the autumn of that year he was detailed to escort some high-ranking officers to Malta. After Nelson's victory at the Battle of the Nile there was no French ship available for them; so they embarked on a sloop from Leghorn. Bad weather and bad seamanship brought them not to Malta but to the Calabrian coast, where their vessel was boarded by a Barbary corsair. The corsair captain was an Albanian from Dulcigno. He had joined a band of corsairs from Tripoli in Libya and had been captured by the Knights of Malta. The French, when they occupied Malta, released him from the galleys, and he went on to Egypt as personal servant to General Duras before escaping and returning to his old profession. His captives, finding that he could speak French, persuaded him to land them on Zante, which, with the other Ionian Islands had been occupied by the French. He would be well rewarded, they promised. Unfortunately, owing to continued bad weather, the two ships were obliged to take refuge in the bay of Navarino. There the corsair learnt that France was at war with the Turks and that the Turks had taken Zante. The corsair captain therefore handed over his captives to the local bey: who decided to send them on to the Pasha at Tripolitza.

Dr Pouqueville spent seven months in captivity at Tripolitza. It was not an arduous captivity. He was allowed to move freely about the town; and it seems that he was able to make journeys under escort to neighbouring spots. He made it his business to find out as much as he could about the country and took copious notes. When finally he returned to France he published in 1805 a work on his travels, dedicated to the Emperor Napoleon. He was later appointed French Consul at Yannina and wrote a history of modern Greece from 1740 to 1824, in four volumes.

Pouqueville's writings had a mixed reception. Lord Byron mocked at his errors when he tried to identify ancient sites. Chateaubriand, who made use of his book of travels, declared that he had described a number of places which, being a prisoner, he could not possibly have visited. The description that he gives of Mistra is full and convincing, and seems to be based on personal experience, unlike his description of the Mani, which he admits that he derived from Maniot friends. Like his predecessors, Pouqueville divides Mistra into four quarters. Of these the castle was now falling into ruin. The upper town, which he calls Mistra itself, was full of narrow, steep and dirty streets, with a number of ruined houses, of which the stones were continually being taken to repair still standing houses. From a distance the buildings were picturesque, especially the brightly coloured Turkish houses. The Greeks had to paint their houses a drab brown. He places the Metropolitan Church in this quarter and dedicates it to the Holy Virgin. His memory must have played him false. He says that the church had recently been restored and was worth a visit. He also mentions the Pantanassa, which he calls the Pandanessi. The convent had been destroyed by the Albanians and the nuns massacred; and though nuns had recovered possession they had as yet to lodge elsewhere.

In the Mesokhorion he noted that the houses, which had numbered three thousand before 1770, were now sparse, with gardens and orchards around them. He says that we need not bother to visit the Church of the Perileptos (sic) or the church that he calls St Paraskevi, by which perhaps he means the Evanghelistria. Since they were sacked, he says, there is nothing left of interest in them. The bazaars and inns were all in the Mesokhorion, where the air, he says, is healthier than in Mistra itself.

To reach the Exokhorion, which is really a town apart, one has, he says, to cross a six-arched bridge over a river that he wrongly calls the Eurotas. The Exokhorion is also called the Evreocastron because it is inhabited by Jews. He estimated that the Jews formed an eighth of the population of Mistra, that is to say, about two thousand souls or a little more. They were, he noted, divided into two groups who would not have anything to do with each other. He calls them Orthodox Jews and Sadducees. It is probable that the division was actually between Sephardim and Ashkenazim, as many of the latter had been for some time past moving from Russia and Poland to find a kindlier atmosphere in the Muslim Turkish world. Pouqueville was told that the Jews all spoke Portuguese amongst themselves; but he may not have met any of the Ashkenazim.

Pouqueville did not believe Mistra to be on the site of ancient Sparta, which he placed on a mound where there were some indeterminate ruins half a league to the east. But he thought that it had been built with the stones of the ancient city, and he remarked that the citizens of Mistra were determined to believe that they lived in Sparta, identifying the market-place, by which he seems to mean the flat space outside the old Palace of the Despots, with the forum of the Spartans. He greatly admired the people of Mistra. The men were tall and handsome and the women very beautiful, as the English topographer Leake also noted, and all of them were free of the subservient mien that characterized too many Peloponnesians. They were on good terms with their Turkish neighbours, who numbered about a third of the population. These Turks, who clearly had a large amount of Greek blood in their veins, usually spoke Greek rather than Turkish, and when they were angry they used Greek oaths, invoking Christ or the Panaghia. They too seemed to him to be excellent folk, of a better type than most other Turkish settlers in the province.

Chateaubriand arrived at Mistra in August 1806. He seems to have read Pouqueville's book, published in Paris in 1805, before he set out. He is unfair about it, accusing Pouqueville of having in the end accepted the local identification of Mistra with Sparta. He himself had been tempted to believe that when he lay in bed at Mistra he was in the spot where Helen and Menelaus had lived; but after a little wandering he came upon the actual site of ancient Sparta. His romantic soul was thrilled; but it was not in fact a novel discovery. The site had been known to previous travellers, including his destructive compatriot, the Abbé Fourment. But no one described it so rhapsodically as did Chateaubriand.

Though he spent several days at Mistra, Chateaubriand made several errors about its topography. Owing, presumably, to his insufficient knowledge of Greek, he calls the upper town, which was badly ruined, he says, the Katokhorion and places the Jewish quarter there. In consequence the stream which divides the Mesokhorion from the Jews' quarter and which he calls the 'Hebriopotamos, Jews' river', has to issue from the town itself. In fact, he was not interested in Mistra. He stayed with a Turkish family in the Mesokhorion; but his only sight-seeing there was to climb to the castle for the view, and to pay an unwilling call upon the Metropolitan at his Palace. He was then taken to see the Metropolitan Church, which he rightly says is dedicated to St Demetrius. He did not think much of it. The inlaid marble floor was dismissed as 'common', while the frescoes 'absolutely resemble the daubings of the school that preceded Perugino'. He did not like its exterior, as he disapproved of domes.

Of the English travellers whom Chateaubriand saw everywhere on the roads of the Peloponnese, not many names have survived of visitors to the vale of Sparta; and we know of none who actually stayed at the English inn at Mistra. Sir William Gell was at Mistra in 1801. He thought that the town looked beautiful from a distance but was seen to be largely in ruins when one came near. He divides it into five parts, giving two names, Tritzella and Parorea, for the area outside of the walls. Edward Dodwell followed in 1806. He noted that it was governed by a voyevod and estimated the population at about seven thousand. But his interest in the town was limited to the sculptured stones and inscriptions, obviously brought from the ruins of Sparta or of Amyclae, that were to be found there. Like most other travellers to Greece at that period, he took little interest in its medieval past.

Chateaubriand mentions two Britishers, whom he calls Swinton and Hawkins, who visited Sparta in 1798. By Swinton he perhaps is referring to John Sibthorpe, who seems to have made the journey with John Hawkins. They barely mention Mistra. The more romantic travellers of the time, such as J. B. S. Morritt, devoted their most eager attention to the Mani, whose inhabitants were traditionally believed to be the descendants of the ancient Spartans: though, to judge from the accounts of the time, they were neither Spartan in their habits, loving any luxury that they could procure, nor in the least Laconic in their speech. They were admired as the only contemporary human survivors of the classical world.

Though classical-minded travellers might ignore Mistra and its ornaments, the city quietly prospered in the early years of the nineteenth century. It was not the city that it had been before 1770. It was now only a small provincial capital. But, as Gell had noted, the valley was fertile and the silk farms were flourishing. When war broke out again between Russia and Turkey in 1787 and the Greeks of Epirus were encouraged by Russian agents to rise in revolt, the Peloponnesians stayed quiet. But the atmosphere throughout the Greek world was changing. The rule of the Sultan was growing increasingly arbitrary and ineffectual; and though many Western travellers dismissed the Greeks as being as corrupt and more servile than their masters, the more observant noted a spirit of impatience and of hope that had not been visible before. The French Revolution brought new ideas of liberty. For a time Napoleon was seen as a likely saviour; but his promises proved to be as cynical and unreliable as those of the Empress Catherine. Then there was a possible ally in Ali Pasha, the formidable lord of Yannina, who, in spite of his equivocal attitude towards the Greeks, seemed eager to aid their revolt in order to embarrass the Sultan and enhance his own independence. There were Greeks, too, who preached revolt. From his comfortable apartment in Paris, Adamantios Korais urged his compatriots to rise against the oppressors, reminding them of the greatness of their ancient past and, less happily, inventing for them an artificial neo-classical language that would, he thought, identify them with their glorious ancestors. More heroic had been the poet Rhegas, whose simple but splendidly eloquent poems gave the same message and who stayed for the most part in his own native land, till in 1798 he went to Vienna to seek help from the rich Greek colony there and was arrested by the Austrian police and shamefully sent by them to Turkey to his death. There was the *Etaireia tôn Philikôn*, the secret society that he had helped to found, with members in the Greek communities inside and outside the Ottoman Empire. It plotted steadily for a great Greek rebellion; indeed, many of its members dreamed of reviving Byzantium. But personal rivalries and differences over policy continually weakened its efficiency.

The Church was in two minds about it all. The Patriarch of Constantinople could not forget his solemn oath of allegiance to the Sultan. Moreover, he had seen the disastrous results of previous revolts. Could he encourage his flock to take a path that would lead almost inevitably to massacre? But as a Greek he longed for freedom. With the Greeks in the provinces, especially in Greece itself, impatient for rebellion and with Korais and his friends denouncing the Church for its subservience to the infidel, he risked losing the devotion of many of his congregations. Indeed, in Greece the monasteries and even some of the bishops were known to give protection to the Klephtic brigands in the north and to anyone who was in trouble with the Ottoman authorities. His older lay advisers, the rich Greeks of the Phanariot quarter in Constantinople, counselled patience. The Ottoman Empire was so rotten that it must soon fall and even the Turks might be ready to let the Greeks take over the government. But the younger Phanariots would not wait; and they were now running the *Etaireia*.

It was planned to start the rising at the end of 1820. One young Phanariot, Alexander Ypsilanti, of a family that had come long ago from Trebizond and claimed descent from the Comneni, was to invade Moldavia from Russia, with Russian support; he was to advance through the Balkans, and all the Balkan Christians would rise to join him. Indeed, the Wallachians were already in rebellion under a national leader, Tudor Vladimirescu. Meanwhile, his brother Demetrius was sent to the Peloponnese to organize rebellion there.

Inevitably, there were delays. Alexander Ypsilanti found that the Russians were not prepared to help an enterprise that they thought foolhardy and one that would embarrass their relations not only with Turkey but also with Austria. But Alexander had collected his force; and it was too late to draw back. Demetrius reported from the Peloponnese growing impatience at the delay. On 22 February (O.S.) Alexander Ypsilanti crossed the River Pruth and marched on Bucharest.

But the Wallachian rebels were there first and would not let him into the city; and there was no sign of any rising of the Bulgarians or the Serbs. In April a large Turkish army moved northward, and Alexander had to retreat towards the Turkish frontier. His troops were routed at a battle at Dragašani. By mid-June the rebellion was over and Alexander was languishing in an Austrian gaol.

In his desire to surprise the Turks, Alexander Ypsilanti had not warned his fellow-plotters of his invasion. When the news reached Constantinople the Patriarch hastily summoned the Holy Synod. Had it come out with a stern denunciation of the revolt its members might have survived. But they could not bring themselves to do so. One or two bishops and a few prominent laymen managed to flee from the city before the Turkish police entered the Patriarchate. A few days later the Patriarch and his senior bishops were hanged at the gate of the Patriarchate; and in the days that followed his leading lay advisers followed him one by one to the gallows.

In the Peloponnese Demetrius Ypsilanti was equally taken by surprise. The Mani was already in a state of revolt; but that was almost endemic. Elsewhere, though the people were impatient, not much had yet been organized. The Turkish governor of the province at once ordered its senior archbishop, the Metropolitan of Patras, with a number of senior Greek notables, to come to Tripolitza for consultation. They knew well that once they were there they would be held as hostages. They set out duly from Patras; but when they reached the Monastery of Agia Lavra near Kalavryta on 25 March (O.S.), the Metropolitan Germanus raised the standard of revolt. The response was immediate and intense. All over the peninsula, bands of peasants and artisans collected under local leaders. They were ill-armed and unorganized; but they were more than the local Turkish garrisons could contain.

It was inevitable that the vale of Sparta should join in the rising. As Pouqueville had noted, the men of Mistra were the least servile of the Peloponnesians. They were ready to look the Turks in the face. Mr Morritt, who despised all Greeks except for the Maniots, told of an old 'Lacedemonian', just returned from Athens, who remarked that he came from a place where nothing was thought dishonourable. The people of Mistra would not be behindhand in joining the struggle for independence.

In many of the Peloponnesian cities the Turks retired to the local fortress to await reinforcements. At Mistra it seems that there was no resistance; and the Turks were allowed to move away in peace. There were none of the terrible scenes that occurred when towards the end of 1821 the insurgent Greeks forced their way into the Turkish provincial capital, Tripolitza, and indulged themselves in wholesale and pitiless massacre. Many of the amiable Turks from Mistra who had taken refuge there must have been amongst the slain.

The history of the Greek War of Independence is long and complex; and the fighting was fierce and bitter. At first, things seemed to go well for the insurgents in the Peloponnese. By the end of 1821 they had captured every town in the peninsula – often with horrible massacres, as at Navarino – with the exception of Nauplia and Patras, and Corone and Methone in the south; and Nauplia was taken in the autumn of 1822. North of the Gulf of Corinth things were not going so well. The revolt of Ali Pasha of Yannina against the Sultan, which had protected the insurgents' flank, was ended by his defeat and death in 1822. A few months later the rebels of western Greece were routed at the Battle of Peta in Epirus. All that was left to them was Missolonghi, where Byron arrived to give them encouragement in 1823 and to die of fever the following April. But when a Turkish army under the Pasha of Drama crossed into the Peloponnese in July 1822, a few days after the Battle of Peta, it was forced to retire in disorder. The Peloponnesians had already set up a provisional government, which met first at Epidaurus. But soon jealousies and rivalries arose, which erupted into civil war. The liberated province was in no position to give help to the cause in northern Greece.

In 1824, fearing to lose the Peloponnese for ever, the Sultan grudgingly begged for the help of his most powerful vassal, Mehmet Ali, Pasha of Egypt. Mehmet Ali had been born in Kavalla in Macedonia, the son of an Albanian adventurer and of the daughter of a local Turkish landowner. He had come to Egypt in 1798, with an Albanian regiment, and had risen rapidly in the Egyptian army, making use of the Mamelukes, whom he later massacred. By 1806 the Sultan had confirmed him as Pasha of Egypt. He at once set about the creation of, first, an efficient fleet and then an efficient army, employing French officers and engineers for the purpose. With their help he made himself master of western Arabia and the Sudan. His growing power alarmed his nominal suzerain, the Sultan; but his help was now needed. In 1822 the Sultan gave him, reluctantly, the Pashalik of Crete, where he suppressed any stirrings for independence amongst the Cretan Greeks. Now he was offered the Pashalik of the Morea and, it seems, of southern Syria, if he would crush the Greek rebellion.

In the autumn of 1824 Mehmet Ali sent a well-equipped fleet and army to Crete under the command of his stepson, Ibrahim, who was proclaimed Pasha of the Morea.

The Greek insurgent admiral Miaoulis, with his fleet of light-armed merchant ships from the islands, managed to harass the Egyptian fleet on its way to Crete and even to capture some transports. But the quarrels among his sea-captains hampered him. He could not prevent the Egyptians from reaching Suda Bay in Crete. Nor could he do anything when the armada left Suda Bay in February and sailed to Methone, where a large and well-disciplined Egyptian army disembarked.

The Greek insurgents had hitherto been faced by Turkish armies which, for all their size, were ill-organized and ill-armed. Ibrahim's army, trained by Frenchmen, most of whom had served under Napoleon, was as efficient as any Western army of the time. As it marched relentlessly through the peninsula the Greek resistance collapsed. From Methone, Ibrahim went to Navarino, to secure its excellent harbour, then through the centre and the north of the province. From Corinth he turned southward into the Argolid. Everywhere along his path, towns and villages were systematically burnt and fields destroyed. The population was slaughtered, except for those who could escape into the mountains and a few who were considered to be valuable prisoners. By September the army reached the vale of Sparta.

Ibrahim's atrocities aroused horror in all Europe, and were to result, in the end, in the Great Powers coming together to take joint action to save the Greeks. In the meantime the British government sent an officer, Captain Hamilton, to intercept the Pasha and arrange if possible for a peaceable exchange of prisoners. Captain Hamilton set out from Nauplia, the only city in the province to be still in Greek hands, hoping to find Ibrahim at Mistra. With Hamilton was an English clergyman called Swan. He left an account of what he saw. As they came down into the valley they noticed from a distance pillars of smoke rising from Mistra; and when they arrived there in the late afternoon of 14 September the houses were in flames and the whole town deserted, except for one cat and one dog. Household possessions were broken and lying about in the streets. Some Greeks who had joined them in the way found them a house in an open space, as yet untouched by the fire. There they bivouacked for the night, expecting every moment to have to leave it for safety. They learnt that Ibrahim had moved out of Mistra that morning after having ordered its destruction. They caught up with him the next day, on the road to Gytheion. He received them graciously enough, but told them that, though he regretted the necessity, he intended to burn and destroy the whole Morea. 'I will not cease,' he repeated, 'till the Morea be a ruin.' Swan describes him as a stout, brown-faced, vulgar-looking man, heavily pock-marked, but with an air of decision. His second-in-command, Suleiman, was a renegade Frenchman who had been aide-de-camp to Marshal Ney and had then escaped to Egypt when the Bourbons were restored. Swan thought him even more vulgar-looking and pock-marked than his master.

On 17 September Captain Hamilton's party passed through Mistra on its way back to Nauplia. It was still smouldering and desolate.

This was the end of Mistra. The destruction had been too great for any restoration to be worthwhile. In the course of the following year Ibrahim's forces once again marched through the province to complete its devastation. It was not till 1827 that the Great Powers, Britain, France and Russia, at last agreed on joint action to save the Peloponnese for the Greeks. On 20 October, in a battle that was sparked off more by accident than design, though the allied admirals were eager for it, the main Egyptian fleet and the main Turkish fleet, which had joined it, were eliminated in the Bay of Navarino.

The Battle of Navarino ensured the emergence of Greece as an independent country. But it was not till August 1828 that Ibrahim was obliged to leave the Peloponnese with his still considerable troops; and a French army under General Maison tried to clean up the country and restore communications and aid in the rebuilding of towns and villages. But Mistra remained a ruin.

At last, in 1832, the Kingdom of Greece was formally established; and in January 1833, its new King Otho, Prince of Bavaria, landed at Nauplia to take over the Kingdom. Otho and his advisers, most of them pedantic Germans, were deeply interested in the classical past, with a contempt for the Middle Ages. After the destruction of Mistra it was necessary to set up a new administrative centre in Laconia; and the authorities decided to refound Sparta. The new city was inaugurated in 1834. Soon the citizens of Mistra, scattered by Ibrahim, found their way there, leaving their old homes on the hill to fall further into ruin. Only the furthermost suburb, the southern part of the Exokhorion, which William Gell had called Parorea, survived to become the small and pleasant town known as Mistra.

Epilogue

FOR MANY DECADES the ruins of Mistra were left to crumble in peace. The nuns returned to the convent of the Pantanassa; but otherwise the old walled city was empty of citizens. Travellers who came to Laconia came to see the remains of ancient Sparta; but they were too sparse to attract many visitors. Travellers occasionally would make their way to Mistra and climb up to the castle to enjoy its spectacular views. But the churches were passed by. No one was interested in them or in what they might contain.

There were one or two exceptions. In 1842 a French architect called Couchaud published a book on Byzantine churches in Greece. He opened his preface by remarking that people were beginning to realize that the art of architecture could contain beauties other than the antique. The book is chiefly concerned with the small churches of Athens. But Couchaud visited Mistra and made a special study of the Church of the Pantanassa. He made drawings not only of the whole building but also of architectural and decorative details; and in his notes he praised the beauty of the frescoes. He seems not to have studied any of the other churches, though he made a drawing of the Church of the Sts Theodore, calling it by mistake the Church of St Nicholas.

Couchaud had few disciples. It was not till the end of the nineteenth century that the art of Mistra was rediscovered and reassessed. For that the chief credit should be given to the French scholar, Gabriel Millet, whose books, published in the early years of this century, revealed the extent and the variety of the frescoes in its churches. Other scholars followed his lead; and the Greek authorities began to undertake the work of conservation that was badly needed. Frescoes have been cleaned and treated, and buildings tactfully restored to ensure their survival. For anyone who has known the site for half a century it is encouraging to see what has been achieved, but frightening to see how much has still to be done.

The Byzantines always loved disputation; and that taste has been inherited by the art historians who deal with Byzantium. Some have dismissed the art of Mistra as being pleasant but provincial; but they for the most part are those to whom the whole art of Byzantium is unsympathetic. Others, realizing that Mistra was a capital city, the residence of princes, to which scholars and artists gladly came from Imperial Constantinople itself, are more ready to appreciate its monuments. To them the argument lies between the respective merits of the frescoes of the Peribleptos and those of the Pantanassa, while to others again the finest are those in the Metropolitan Church. These differences are a tribute to the work of the artists of Mistra.

The city had already received its greatest literary accolade. It was in Mistra that Goethe placed, in the second part of his *Faust*, the meeting of Faust with Helen of Troy. Goethe never visited Greece, and his knowledge of Greek topography was shaky. Mistra to him was a forlorn ridge that rose northward in Sparta's rear behind Taygetus. But his sense of symbolism was sure. There could be no better site for the meeting of the classical and the medieval world than this city, built close to the ruins of ancient Sparta, this medieval city where classical learning was so lovingly preserved and taught. From this meeting came the New Learning of the Renaissance; and in this meeting the philosophers of Mistra played a large and valued part.

The old city is deserted now, except for the kindly nuns who maintain, in the convent of the Pantanassa, the eternal traditions of the Orthodox faith, and for the helpful guardians and the officers of the small museum down by the Metropolitan Church. When one leaves the little modern town outside the old walls and passes by the statue that it has erected to the most heroic of its princes, the Emperor Constantine, who fell before the walls of Constantinople, one reaches a world that must be peopled by figments of the imagination. But, for those to whom history is not just a matter of dry and dusty records, the imagination offers a splendid choice, whether it be of warriors or artists, of gracious ladies or learned philosophers, of the Villehardouin lords revelling in the loveliness of the countryside, of the dark-bearded Despots in their ceremonial robes discussing with their architects and artists how to add to the city's glories, or of the great philosopher Plethon himself talking to his pupils, while the Lady Cleope leaned from her litter to greet him as she passed: or, later, of the Ottoman pashas lording it in the princes' seats, so courteous to foreign visitors and so contemptuous of their Christian subjects: or just of the simple craftsmen and artisans, and the peasants coming in to the market, whose descendants we may still see driving their goats through the steep and narrow alleys, while behind them are the peaks and chasms of Taygetus and spread out before them the incomparable beauty of the hollow vale of Sparta.

132

Bibliographical Note
Genealogical Table
Index

Bibliographical Note

Of the original sources on which a history of Mistra must be based there is none which makes the city its main theme. But the number of sources which refer to Mistra or are relevant to its history is enormous. In the excellent bibliography provided by D. Zakythinos in his *Le Despotat grec de Morée*, vol. I, published in 1932, some 85 original narrative sources are cited, with 7 unedited manuscripts and some 60 collections of documents. Not all of these deal with Mistra itself, but all of them concern the Peloponnese at a time when Mistra was its most important centre.

The chief source for the history of the Peloponnese in the thirteenth century is a chronicle which exists in three versions, all probably derived from an original version which is lost. One is written in doggerel verse in a local Greek dialect, full of words of Frankish origin, entitled *The Chronicle of the Morea*. (The best edition was published in Athens in 1940 by P. P. Kalomaros.) It tells of events as far as 1292. There is a version in old French, *Le Livre de la conqueste de la Princée de l'Amorie* (ed. J. Longnon, Paris, 1911), which goes as far as 1304. Then there is a version in Aragonese, *Libro de los fechos et conquistas del Principado de la Morea* (ed. A. Morel-Fatio, Geneva, 1885), which takes the story on to 1377 but is less detailed as regards the thirteenth century. There is also a short Italian version which is an abridgement of the Greek. The chronicle in all its versions is heavily prejudiced in favour of the Franks and against the Greeks. Some of its details are demonstrably incorrect; but it all gives a vigorous and vivid picture of the life of the time. There are no later Western chronicles that deal more than marginally with the Peloponnese, though some are important for certain episodes, such as that of Ramon Muntaner (*Chronica*, ed. K. Lanz, Stuttgart, 1844) for the story of the Catalan Company. The sources for the later history of the Principality of Achaea are to be found mainly in the archives of the Angevin Kingdom of Naples, and in Venetian chronicles and archives.

To the Byzantine chroniclers and historians, Peloponnesian affairs tend, at first at least, to be peripheral. George Pachymer reports the Byzantine recovery of part of the Peloponnese after the Battle of Pelagonia. In the fourteenth century the ex-Emperor John Cantacuzenus has more to say about Mistra; he had appointed one of his sons to be its Despot, and in his old age, when he was writing his History, he paid several visits there. His contemporary, Nicephorus Gregoras, has not much to say in his History about Mistra, though he maintained a correspondence with the Despots Manuel and Matthew. The final generation of Byzantine historians is more informative. Indeed, Mistra was relatively much more important to the Byzantine world in their time. Ducas has the least to say. Of the others, Laonicus Chalcocondyles was an Athenian and concerned with affairs in the Greek peninsula; Critobulus, the apologist of the Turkish conquest, was a friend of the last Despot of Mistra, Demetrius; and George Sphrantzes spent most of his working life in the service of Constantine Palaeologus. In addition to the Byzantine historians' works, there are a number of letters and funeral orations, which shed further light, as do the political tracts by Plethon. The histories of Pachymer, John Cantacuzenus and Gregoras are published in the Bonn *Corpus scriptorum historiae*

Byzantinae in 1835, 1828–32 and 1829–55 respectively. The best edition of Chalcocondyles is by E. Darko (Budapest, 1922–7) and of Ducas, Critobulus and Sphrantzes by V. Grecu (Bucharest, 1958, 1962 and 1968). Many of the shorter sources are to be found in S. Lambros, *Palaeologeia kai Peloponnesiaka* (in Greek), published in Athens, 1912–30, and in K. N. Sathas, *Bibliotheca graeca medii aevi* (Venice/Paris, 1872–94).

Of the secondary sources the most important for the medieval period is D. A. Zakythinos, *Le Despotat grec de Morée*, of which the first volume, dealing with the political history, was published in Paris in 1932 and the second volume, dealing with life and institutions, in Athens in 1953. William Miller's *The Latins in the Levant* (London, 1908) is still of immense value; and there is a useful chapter by K. M. Setton, 'The Latins in Greece and the Aegean', in vol. IV, pt 1 (1966 edn) of the *Cambridge Medieval History*. For the intellectual life of Mistra the most complete study is by F. Masai, *Plethon et le Platonisme de Mistra* (Paris, 1956). Extracts from Plethon's own writings, giving his political views, can be found in E. Barker, *Social and Political Thought in Byzantium* (Oxford, 1957).

For the art of Mistra the basic work is G. Millet, *Monuments byzantins de Mistra* (Paris, 1910). A. Orlandos's work, *Palaces and Houses in Mistra* (in Greek, Athens, 1937), is also important. Every modern work on

Byzantine art contains a section on Mistra, though the authors do not all agree about the sources and the quality of the painting.

The history of Mistra under the Turks is not nearly as well documented as the medieval period. There has been no general history of Greece under the Turks since George Finlay's *History of Greece under Othoman and Venetian Domination*, published in London in 1856 and reissued in the last volumes of his *History of Greece, BC 146 to AD 1864*, edited in five volumes by H. F. Tozer (Oxford, 1877), a book which is full of interesting material but is out of date in many places and all marked by Finlay's idiosyncratic views and prejudices. There are two useful chapters in William Miller's *Essays on the Latin Orient* (Cambridge, 1921) which deal with Turkish Greece and the Venetian Revival. The Greeks themselves have tended to neglect this period of their history, considering it somewhat inglorious. They are wrong, for it pays tribute to the tenacity and often to the heroism of their race and their traditions. There are, as far as I know, no original sources in Greek that deal with Mistra and Laconia. Such works as the Chronicle of Galaxidi or the so-called Chronicle of Dorotheus of Monemvasia occasionally mention the Mani but never Mistra. We are dependent on Venetian records, which are fairly plentiful up till the final evacuation of the Morea by the Republic in 1718. It is possible that more information could be unearthed by scholars able to dig into the Ottoman archives. For the eighteenth century and early nineteenth the most valuable information comes from the accounts of Western travellers who visited Greece. I have made use of several of them in the course of this book. The first Englishman to describe Mistra from personal experience was Bernard Randolph, whose *Present State of the Morea* was published at Oxford in 1686. Many of the British travellers who came in some numbers to Greece during the following century and a half have their accounts published in two volumes edited by the Rev. Robert Walpole, himself an assiduous traveller, *Memoirs relating to European and Asiatic Turkey* and *Travels to various Countries of the East* (London, 1818 and 1820). These contain several references to Mistra. The fullest account is, however, by the French traveller, Pouqueville, in his *Voyage en Morée*, published in Paris in 1805. He was followed by Chateaubriand, though the latter was more concerned with ancient Sparta than with Mistra. I have made use of the English version of his *Travels in Greece* (translated by F. Shoberl, London, 1811). The two distinguished British topographers Sir William Gell and Captain W. M. Leake did not publish their accounts till some time after their Peloponnesian journeys were made. Gell, who was there in 1804–6, did not issue his *Narrative of a Journey in the*

Morea till 1823, when he hoped that it would discourage support for the Greek Revolution. Leake's *Travels in the Morea* did not appear till 1830, with a supplement, *Peloponnesiaca*, in 1840. Both deal rather summarily with Mistra, as does William Mure of Caldwell in his *Journal of a Tour in Greece* (London, 1842). He visited Mistra after the foundation of new Sparta. In the vast literature on the Greek War of Independence the only work to mention Mistra in any detail is the Rev. C. Swan's *Voyage to the Eastern Mediterranean* (London, 1826), which gives the description that I have quoted of Ibrahim Pasha's burning of the city.

There are short descriptive books on Mistra by Marie Sotiriou, *Mistra, une ville morte* (Athens, 1956), by Manolis Chadzidakis, who has himself worked on the preservation of the monuments, *Mistra, History, Monuments, Art* (in Greek, Athens, 1956), and by Panyotis Kanellopoulos, *Mistra, das byzantinische Pompeji* (Munich, 1962). The Soviet historian, I. P. Medvedev, has written a scholarly history of Mistra in the Middle Ages, *Mistra* (in Russian, Moscow, 1973).

A short but useful guide to Mistra by Nikos V. Georgiades, translated by Brian de Jongh, can be bought on the spot. There is a good account of the ruins in de Jongh's excellent *Companion Guide to Southern Greece* (London, 1972).

The Palaeologus and Cantacuzenus Families

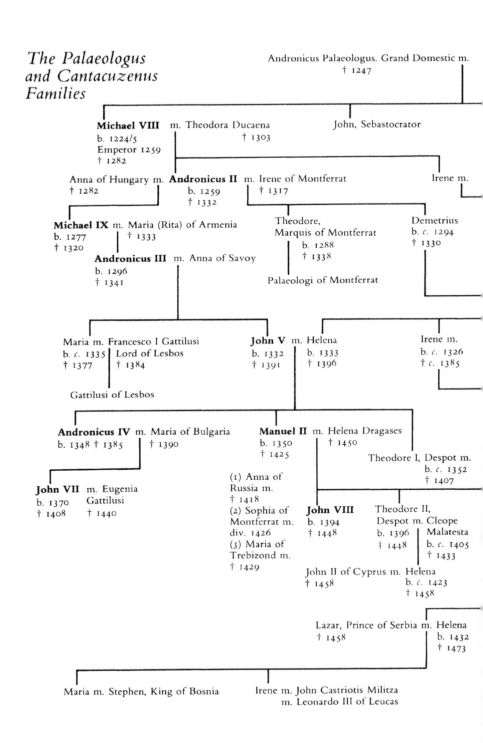

Andronicus Palaeologus. Grand Domestic m.
† 1247

Michael VIII m. Theodora Ducaena
b. 1224/5 † 1303
Emperor 1259
† 1282

John, Sebastocrator

Anna of Hungary m. **Andronicus II** m. Irene of Montferrat
† 1282 b. 1259 † 1317
† 1332

Irene m.

Michael IX m. Maria (Rita) of Armenia
b. 1277 † 1333
† 1320

Theodore,
Marquis of Montferrat
b. 1288
† 1338

Demetrius
b. c. 1294
† 1330

Andronicus III m. Anna of Savoy
b. 1296
† 1341

Palaeologi of Montferrat

Maria m. Francesco I Gattilusi
b. c. 1335 Lord of Lesbos
† 1377 † 1384

John V m. Helena
b. 1332 b. 1333
† 1391 † 1396

Irene m.
b. c. 1326
† c. 1385

Gattilusi of Lesbos

Andronicus IV m. Maria of Bulgaria
b. 1348 † 1385 † 1390

Manuel II m. Helena Dragases
b. 1350 † 1450
† 1425

Theodore I, Despot m.
b. c. 1352
† 1407

John VII m. Eugenia
b. 1370 Gattilusi
† 1408 † 1440

(1) Anna of
Russia m.
† 1418
(2) Sophia of
Montferrat m.
div. 1426
(3) Maria of
Trebizond m.
† 1429

John VIII
b. 1394
† 1448

Theodore II,
Despot m. Cleope
b. 1396 Malatesta
† 1448 b. c. 1405
† 1433

John II of Cyprus m. Helena
† 1458 b. c. 1423
† 1458

Lazar, Prince of Serbia m. Helena
† 1458 b. 1432
† 1473

Maria m. Stephen, King of Bosnia

Irene m. John Castriotis Militza
m. Leonardo III of Leucas

Theodora, daughter of Alexius Palaeologus and Irene Angelina Comnena

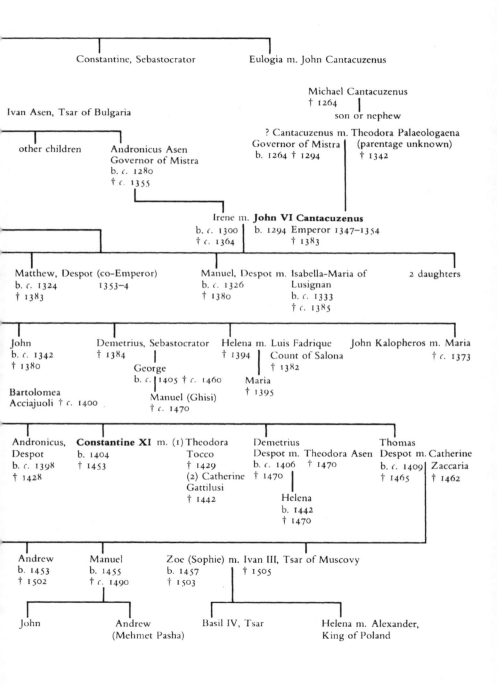

Index

Note: names of peoples and places that occur continually in the text, such as Greeks and Arabs, are omitted from the index.